JUNG AND ALCHEMY

A Path To Individuation

I0130161

Murray Stein

CHIRON PUBLICATIONS • ASHEVILLE, NORTH CAROLINA

© 2025 by Chiron Publications. All rights reserved. No part of this publication may be reproduced, stored in a retrieval system, or transmitted, in any form by any means, electronic, mechanical, photocopying, recording, or otherwise, without the prior written permission of the publisher, Chiron Publications, P.O. Box 19690, Asheville, N.C. 28815-1690.

This work may not be used without permission for artificial intelligence training or development of machine learning language models.

www.ChironPublications.com

Interior design by Danijela Mijailovic
Printed primarily in the United States of America

Front cover painting, "Mercurius"©, by Diane Stanley

ISBN 978-1-68503-600-3 paperback
ISBN 978-1-68503-601-0 hardcover
ISBN 978-1-68503-602-7 electronic
ISBN 978-1-68503-603-4 limited edition paperback
ISBN 978-1-68503-604-1 limited edition hardcover

Table of Contents

Acknowledgments   v

Lecture One – Introduction to Jung's Writings
on Alchemy   1

Lecture Two – Alchemical Symbols as States
of Mind   29

Lecture Three – Alchemy as Active Imagination   53

Lecture Four – Alchemy in a Dream Series   71

Lecture Five – The Alchemy of Transcendence in
Relationship   89

Lecture Six – The Culmination of Jung's Opus:
Mysterium Coniunctionis   119

Bibliography   139

Acknowledgements

I wish to express gratitude to many, and especially to the students who have patiently listened to my lectures on alchemy for more than 50 years. They have been an inspiration and a challenge. When I began to explore *Mysterium Coniunctionis* with a small group of eager students at the Houston Jung Center in 1973, it was a new text to me as well as to them. We learned together. Having nearly worn out my copy of this volume and the other of Jung's published writings on alchemy in the years since then, I am still discovering nuggets of gold in the enchanting depths of Jung's alchemical mind with every new reading. Many other students have participated in the meantime, notably Wendy Wilmot and Mary Tomlinson, with whom I have engaged in bi-weekly discussions of *Mysterium* and other alchemy texts for more than a decade.

Also, my heartfelt thanks go to Diane Stanley, who performed the heroic task of transcribing and arranging the spoken words of the lectures from recordings into a manuscript that I could work on at my leisure. Her help was much more than only a time-saver; it was also a key factor in the eventual creation of this book as it now stands before the reader. Without her help and constant encouragement, I would not have brought this work to its present publishable form.

I wish to add a word, too, about the image on the book's cover—an original stained-glass window created by the artist Diane Stanley. The image is of Mercurius, agent of transformation in all alchemical processes. Mercurius carries a child in his womb, indicating both his hermaphroditic nature and his forecast of the future. In the picture, he is Wind (spirit, *pneuma*)—guide and inspirator of the entire process.

Also, most worthy of gratitude are my companions at Chiron: Steve Buser, Len Cruz, and Jennifer Fitzgerald. They have been constant presences on this journey to publication. To them I owe a huge debt of gratitude.

And finally, but not by any means least, my gratitude to Valerie Appleby for her meticulous care with the words and phrases I committed to paper. It is to her credit that the text is as polished as it is.

Lecture One
Introduction to Jung's Writings on Alchemy

To prepare for these lectures, I looked back through notes from other courses and realized once again how important the study of alchemy was for Jung in his later years. As he wrote in his last major book, *Mysterium Coniunctionis*, "alchemy provides the psychology of the unconscious with a meaningful historical basis."[1] For Jung, the value of alchemy was that it gave him meaningful orientation for his work as a depth psychologist. I will begin these lectures by placing Jung's alchemical studies in the context of his life and work.

Karl (later changed to Carl) Gustav Jung was born in a small village in Switzerland on July 26, 1875, and lived the first 25 years of his life mostly in the vicinity of Basel, where he attended grammar school, Gymnasium, and the ancient university located there. Jung commented quite extensively on his youth in the first chapters of

---

[1] Jung, *Mysterium Coniunctionis*, xiii.

Memories, Dreams, Reflections (hereinafter *MDR*), the autobiographical work he created with the assistance of Aniela Jaffé, his secretary and close collaborator in his later years. It is to Jaffé's credit that we have this marvellous testament to Jung's inner life. I will not speak further about those early years here, only to say that *MDR* contains much fascinating material about Jung's childhood.

The second stage of his life, which I think of as his apprenticeship and refer to as the "Early Jung" period, began in 1895 when, at the age of 20, he entered the University of Basel to study medicine. His earliest available writings, now published, are five lectures that he delivered to the Zofingiaverein, a Swiss student fraternity, during his term as president of the Basel chapter. In these early papers, we see the young man lecturing not on medical topics but on psychology, religion, and philosophy. As a teenager, he had begun reading the works of Kant and Schopenhauer (see *MDR*), and at this time, he was also grappling with the ideas of Nietzsche and Albrecht Ritschl—great thinkers and leading cultural figures in the German-speaking world and beyond. Already as a youth and a medical student, Jung was signalling what would become his primary vocation in life—exploration of the psyche.

In 1900, Jung graduated medical school and began his study of psychiatry in Zürich at the famous Burghölzli Clinic. During his residency there, under the direction of the chief psychiatrist Eugen Bleuler, he began publishing technical papers and books in psychiatry and psychology. His research using the Word Association Experiment (WAE) dates to this period, and his involvement with Freud and psychoanalysis also began at this time. The first five volumes of the *Collected Works* represent Jung's publications in these early years, spanning 1902 to 1913.

While working at the Burghözli Clinic, Jung married Emma Rauschenbach (in 1903), and the couple's first three children were born during their time occupying an apartment on clinic grounds. In 1908, they were able to build a house for themselves and their growing family in the village of Küsnacht on Lake Zurich, and in 1909 they moved into it. There, Jung opened his private psychoanalytic practice while continuing to work and teach at the university hospital until early 1914. The "Early Jung" period concluded with his resignation from the University of Zurich and his final break with Freud, also in 1914.

The "Middle Jung" period followed, spanning the ages of 38 to 55 (1913–1930). It opened with Jung in a severe midlife crisis. Midlife is a transitional phase in the individuation process—a time that Jung referred to in *MDR* as a "confrontation with the unconscious." He recorded his experiences of this confrontation in his journals (the *Black Books*) and subsequently transcribed his notes—rendered in exquisite calligraphic script—into what has come to be known as *The Red Book* (originally titled *Liber Novus*). During this period, Jung was active in his practice as a psychoanalyst, while also lecturing, traveling, and writing. This was perhaps his most creative period, although not his most productive for publishing. The implications of what he discovered during this period would be worked out in the years to follow, leading up to his death in 1961.

In the midst of his intense inner work with figures of the unconscious, and as World War I raged throughout Europe, the Psychological Club was formed. This was conceived of as an experiment in communitas and was meant to counterbalance the one-sided introversion induced in patients by the methods Jung used in his practice of psychoanalysis. Club members consisted primarily of Jung's analysands and some close members of his inner circle, including Emma Jung (the Club's first president) and Toni Wolff. At the Club's scientific meetings, Jung gave initial expression to his emerging ideas, developing his key theoretical constructs of the transcendent function (as formed through active imagination), psychological types, archetypes, and the collective unconscious. Some of his thinking on these concepts had already begun toward the end of his apprenticeship with Freud, but in the congenial atmosphere of the Club, he was able to take his ideas much further. *Psychological Types*, published in 1921, summarizes almost everything he knew about psychology at that time. In the concluding chapter of that work, he included a lexicon of terms and defined their meanings as assigned to them in his usage. This is the most important work Jung published during his middle period. While *The Red Book: Liber Novus* was not published in his lifetime, it could be considered the seedbed of all that was to follow.

In this period, too, Jung made important connections with a number of eminent scholars and thinkers, among them the German Sinologist Richard Wilhelm, whom he met in Darmstadt, Germany at Count Keyserling's School of Wisdom in the early 1920s. Wilhelm played the hermetic role of getting Jung involved in the study of alchemy, which would occupy him for the rest of his life and take a central position in the works he published during his later period (1930–1961).

Jung also travelled extensively during his middle period—most significantly to Africa in 1925—and began building his tower at Bollingen. This period concluded between 1928 and 1930 (ages 53 to 55), and the "Late Jung" period began with his newfound interest in alchemy, following his study and composition of a "Commentary" on *The Secret of the Golden Flower*. At the heart of this late period was Jung's work on alchemy and its relevance to psychological theory, psychoanalytic practice, and Western culture. Whereas the middle period saw Jung discover his personal myth, his late period focused on the development of a new myth for Western culture and the world.

In 1928, Jung painted a mandala image in *The Red Book*, beneath which he inscribed: "When I painted this image, which showed the golden well-fortified castle, Richard Wilhelm sent me from Frankfort the Chinese thousand-year-old text of the golden castle, the embryo of the immortal body."[2] This turned out to be a pivotal moment in Jung's intellectual life and his conception of the unconscious. Studying this ancient Chinese text, he found some surprising parallels and similarities to his own active imagination experiences, as recorded in *The Red Book*, and his work with patients. This gave him a hint of a larger context, which he referred to as the collective unconscious. In *MDR*, he wrote that, for the first time, he felt as if he had broken out of his isolation and felt reassured that he was not as eccentric as he had feared. He discovered that the ancient Chinese alchemists had been doing something quite similar to him, and their experiences were not so different from his own. Jung concluded from this that, in doing his inner work in isolation in his library, he may have made contact with a level of the psyche common to all humanity—the collective unconscious. This gave him confidence that he was on the right track in creating a psychology that was not merely personal, but universal.

Before encountering *The Secret of the Golden Flower* and alchemy, Jung reported in *MDR* that he had a series of dreams that repeatedly dealt with the same theme—discovering unknown rooms or wings of his house.[3] Each time, he wondered in the dream why he didn't know about these rooms beforehand. Through his

---

[2] Jung, *The Red Book*, 320, n. 307.
[3] Jung, *Memories, Dreams, Reflections*, 202.

work with patients, Jung discovered that many people have dreams in which they open a door and discover a whole new section of their house that they didn't know existed, or they find another level beneath the basement, or they stumble upon a room or series of rooms that were previously unknown to them. Indeed, this is a well-known, frequent dream motif. Jung wrote that he experienced this motif several times before finally dreaming that he managed to reach the other wing of the house and walk into it. There, he discovered an impressive library dating back to the sixteenth and seventeenth centuries, containing large folio volumes bound in pigskin. Among them were a number of books embellished with copper engravings of a strange character. This library, which he described as a collection of medieval incunabula and sixteenth century prints, fascinated him.

This dream occurred a couple of years prior to Jung's growing fascination with alchemy. Later, he recognized the symbols on the books: they were alchemical. Jung knew that the unknown wing of the house symbolized a part of his personality of which he was not yet conscious. The library specifically referred to alchemy: "Some fifteen years later I had assembled a library very like the one in the dream."[4] It seems Jung was destined to study this subject. It had the deepest personal meaning for him. In *MDR*, he wrote: "I regard my work

---

[4] Ibid.

in alchemy as a sign of my inner relationship to Goethe. Goethe's secret was that he was in the grip of that process of archetypal transformation which has gone on through the centuries… I myself am haunted by the same dream, and from my eleventh year I have been launched upon a single enterprise which is my 'main business.'"[5] That "main business" for Jung was "to penetrate into the secret of the personality," and alchemy gave him the key.

In *MDR,* Jung carefully described how he gradually began delving into alchemy. His first exposure came through a book published in 1914 by his psychoanalytic colleague Herbert Silberer, *Problems of Mysticism and Its Symbolism.* Jung wrote that he read the book shortly after its publication, but found it of little interest at the time. It wasn't until 1928, following his "Commentary" on *The Secret of the Golden Flower,* that Jung resolved to undertake a serious study of alchemy. The first alchemical volume he bought was *Auriferae Volumina Duo* (1593)—a collection of classic alchemy texts in Latin. Paging through it, he was completely baffled and could make nothing of its strange terms and arcane symbolism. Nevertheless, he continued building his alchemical collection as more books became available from booksellers. When he received the sixteenth century text *Rosarium Philosophorum,* he began to notice the repetition of certain words and phrases: *solve et coagula,*

---

[5] Ibid., 206.

unum vas, lapis, prima materia, Mercurius.[6] As time went on, these terms became very familiar to him—as they have also become to us, his readers. Jung recounted that he began to systematically review the texts, underlining recurrent words and compiling an index of alchemical terms and phrases. This index, eventually comprising eight volumes of extracts, drawings, and terminology, later became his basic resource as he proceeded to penetrate into the mysterious world of alchemical imagination and use it for his own purposes.[7]

It became evident to Jung that the alchemists were among his most important spiritual ancestors, with whom he could identify closely. When he wrote about the sixteenth century physician and alchemist Paracelsus, for instance, he felt deep kinship with this Swiss forebear. He recognized in the alchemists' writings themes and symbols that were familiar to him from his experiences in active imagination and his work with patients, and he came to regard the alchemists as the forerunners of analytical psychology. Jung engaged extensively with alchemical texts for approximately twenty-five years, culminating in the publication of his final major work on alchemy, *Mysterium Coniunctionis,* in 1955.

In those years of engagement with alchemy, terrible things were happening in the political and

---

[6] Ibid., 205.
[7] Shamdasani, *C.G. Jung: A Biography in Books.* See 172ff.

financial spheres: the rise of Nazism in Germany, the Great Depression, the war, the Holocaust. Sitting in his library and immersing himself in the texts and symbols of his alchemical books must have offered Jung some solace—an intellectual refuge among kindred minds. What he found so companionable about them, also, was their hereticism—albeit a quiet hereticism, for the most part, when it came to theological matters. Indeed, the alchemists were not conventional people. Through them, Jung also delved into Jewish mysticism (some of the alchemists were Kabbalists). It was in these heretical and occult traditions that Jung found company with like-minded thinkers.

In *MDR*, Jung recounted a dream he had in 1926, shortly before receiving Wilhelm's translation of *The Secret of the Golden Flower*, which had an important bearing on his engagement with alchemy. In the dream, he was traveling in Italy with a companion and ended up in Verona, where they entered the courtyard of a large manor house. The manor resembled the Louvre Palace in Paris, with an inner courtyard surrounded by impressive buildings. The coachman drove in through a gate, and at the far end of the courtyard they could see a second gate. Suddenly, both gates slammed shut and Jung realized they were locked in. The coachman leapt down from his seat and exclaimed: "Now we are caught in the seventeenth century!" Jung thought to himself, "Well, what's that! But what is there to do about it? Now we shall be caught for years." Then the consoling thought came to him:

"Someday, years from now, I shall get out again."[8] And indeed, it took him thirty years to get out! Jung spent a lot of time in the world of alchemy. As he wrote, the seventeenth century was very significant, as it was more or less the high point of European alchemy.

A survey of Jung's references to alchemists throughout his *Collected Works* reveals a wide range of figures, spanning from the early centuries of the Common Era to the nineteenth century. Among these, the following are considered most important:

> First Century
>> Hermes Trismegistus
>> Maria Prophetissa
>> Komarios
>
> Second Century – Pseudo-Democritus
> Fourth Century – Zosimos of Panopolis
> Fifth Century – Morienus
> Seventh Century – Kalid (Khalid ibn Jazid ibn Muawiyah)
> Eighth Century – Geber (Jabir ibn Hayyan)
> Tenth Century – Senior (Muhammed ibn Umail)
> Twelfth Century – Artephius
> Thirteenth Century
>> Albertus Magnus
>> Arnold de Vilanova
>> Roger Bacon

---

[8] Jung, *Memories, Dreams, Reflections*, 203.

Raymound Lully

Fourteenth Century – Joannes de Rupescissa (or Jean de Roquetaillade)

Fifteenth Century

    Christian Rosencreutz

    Agrippa von Nettesheim

    Bernard of Treviso

    Marsilio Ficino

    George Ripley

Sixteenth Century

    Jakob Boehme

    John Dee

    Theobald de Hoghelande

    Gerhard Dorn

    Heinrich Khunrath

    Andreas Libavius

    Melchior

    Samuel Norton

    Orthelius

    Paracelsus

    Josephus Quercetanus

    Martin Ruland

    Michael Sendivogius

    Solomon Trismosin

    Agrippa Von Nettesheim

Seventeenth Century

    Herbrandt Jamsthaler

    Michael Maier

    Johan Daniel Mylius

> Philalethes (George Starkey)
> Eighteenth Century – Abraham Eleazar
> Nineteenth Century – Goethe

These figures held particular significance for Jung. They were his companions, and their names recur frequently in his alchemical writings.

From the first century of the Common Era, there is the famous mythical figure Hermes Trismegistus (Thrice-Great Hermes), who, according to tradition, wrote *The Emerald Tablet*—one of the basic documents of alchemy. There is also the equally mythical Maria Prophetissa, to whom Jung frequently refers in his *Collected Works*, who described the process of development from one to four in the famous formula: "One becomes two, two becomes three, and out of the third comes the one as the fourth." Jung interpreted this as the basic formula for the individuation process.

The origins of alchemy are undoubtedly to be found in the early science of metallurgy.[9] Hephaestus and similar mythical characters worked with metals, using fire to melt and fuse them in the pursuit of stronger weapons and tools. In the course of their work, these metallurgists discovered all kinds of strange properties within the metals, allowing them to transform and blend with others. Another source of alchemy is thought to lie in the ancient Egyptian mummification rituals, aiming at the preservation

---

[9] See Mircea Eliade, *The Forge and the Crucible*.

13

and immortalization of the body. Likewise, there is a strong theme in alchemy of attaining immortality through the opus. Alchemy also entered pharmacology, of course, in the search for the *alexipharmakon*—the medicine that heals all wounds and ailments. The quest for health and immortality is a main theme in *The Secret of the Golden Flower*, which teaches that, through meditation, one can create a diamond body—a spiritual substance that is both incorruptible and immortal. Certainly, the attainment of good health was a secondary goal of the alchemists.

The first century figures in Western alchemy (among them Hermes Trismegistus, Komarios, and Maria Prophetissa) are quasi-mythical personalities, as nothing is known about them as historical persons. However, these mysterious figures left behind a legacy of sayings and formulas that were frequently referenced by later alchemists, as well as by Jung. In contrast, Pseudo-Democritus of the second century and Zosimos of Panopolis of the fourth century are more firmly situated within historical context, and these figures also held great importance to Jung. Jung devoted an entire essay to Zosimos, whose visionary writings revolved around themes of initiation and transformation through dismemberment, engendering spiritual enlightenment.[10] Jung regarded these visions as symbolic of the individuation process, mirroring the symbolic material

---

[10] Jung, "The Visions of Zosimos," *Collected Works* (hereinafter cited in text as *CW)* 13.

he observed in the dreams and active imaginations of his patients in the modern day.

Kalid is an Arab alchemist from the seventh century whom frequently Jung referenced, and Geber, who wrote an important work on alchemy in the eighth century, has the dubious distinction of serving as the etymological source of the word *gibberish* ("alchemy is gibberish"; i.e., nonsense). In the tenth century, the alchemist referred to as Senior (Muhammad ibn Umail) appeared, whom Jung often quoted.[11] In the thirteenth century, some very important writers on alchemy emerged, including Albertus Magnus, the teacher of Thomas Aquinas. Jung also frequently referenced Roger Bacon, a very important figure in the history of science, and Raymond Lully, a Spanish alchemist.

Jung only referenced one fourteenth century alchemist: Joannes de Rupescissa (or Jean de Roque-taillade). However, in the fifteenth century, several important figures entered the scene, including George Ripley, author of the *Cantilena*, upon which Jung commented extensively in *Mysterium Coniunctionis*.

By the sixteenth century, alchemy was approaching its height in the West, and many figures from this period appear prominently and frequently in Jung's works. Jakob Boehme, for instance, was a pillar of a countercultural and mystical tradition taking hold in the West, and an

---

[11] M.-L. von Franz's last book was a commentary on Senior's work, *Hall Ar-Rumuz* ("*Clearing of Enigmas*").

important figure for Jung. Also important was Agrippa von Nettesheim, the German occultist, theologian, and alchemist. Likewise, John Dee, the renowned English alchemist, scientist, and advisor to Queen Elisabeth I, was frequently cited, as well as de Hoghelande. Gerhard Dorn, whose work permeates Jung's writings on alchemy, was arguably Jung's most esteemed alchemical author. Dorn features prominently in the final chapter of *Mysterium Coniunctionis*, which articulates Jung's final and most comprehensive vision of individuation as a psychological and spiritual development process. Heinrich Conrad Khunrath and Melchior, both esteemed and influential figures of the time, frequently appear in Jung's writings. Paracelsus, however, appears to have occupied a uniquely personal place for Jung. A fellow Swiss countryman, as well as an alchemist, physician, philosopher and theologian, Paracelsus wove together themes from natural science, medicine, religion, ancient philosophy, and alchemy. This fascinated Jung, offering him a model for linking psychology and spirituality without repudiating his own religious tradition, Christianity. In 1941, Jung delivered two celebrated lectures on Paracelsus in Einsiedeln to commemorate the 400th anniversary of his death. Also notable from this fertile century is Solomon Trismosin, author of the exquisitely illustrated *The Splendor Solis*— regarded as one of the most brilliant among all gems in the alchemical literature.

Then we come to the seventeenth century, where Jung found himself trapped in his dream of 1926, referenced above. Here, he found himself among notable alchemists of the era, including Michael Maier—a figure for whom Jung held particular admiration and whom he studied in depth. While alchemy reached its zenith in the sixteenth century, the seventeenth century witnessed a decisive shift: science and alchemy began to diverge, and, with the emergence of empirical investigations and laboratory experimentation, chemistry was established as an independent physical science. The seventeenth century marked a turning point in Western intellectual history—one in which the cultural authority of religion gave way to the rationalism of the Enlightenment and the rise of modern science. As a consequence, alchemy, with its admixtures of philosophy and religion, was increasingly marginalized, and ultimately relegated to the library, where it continued to inspire speculative thought. In contrast, the laboratory—once a site of symbolic projection—came to serve only the demands of empirical science.

What Jung appreciated so much about classical alchemy was that the alchemists had not split psyche and spirit off from matter. They were thus able to work with the spirit present in physical materials, including ore and plants. To them, there was no division between inner (mind) and outer (matter). Jung thought we could learn something from that—not for the purposes of laboratory chemistry, but for our own psychological work.

There is a famous alchemy picture spanning two plates. On the first plate, one can see alchemists standing in a library among many books and discussing recipes and theory. The second plate depicts a laboratory worker stripped down to his loin cloths as he attends the fire in a furnace, sweating profusely as he works with the materials.

A practicing alchemist would go back and forth between the library and the laboratory, both consulting their books and tending the flame. Jung associated this cyclical pattern to analysis and psychological work: The diligent analyst goes back and forth between studying and practicing, practicing on oneself and practicing with patients, and studying the books. They deepen their theoretical understanding while staying very much in contact with the material of the psyche. This prevents their understanding of depth psychology from becoming a purely academic enterprise.

In the eighteenth century, the figure of Abraham Eleazar emerged. Though it is uncertain whether he was in fact Jewish, his alchemical writings incorporate elements of Jewish philosophy and theology—particularly the Kabbalah. In *Mysterium Coniunctionis*, Jung commented extensively on a passage by Eleazar.

Among the nineteenth century alchemists, Goethe held particular significance for Jung as both a literary and an alchemical figure. A family rumour claimed that Jung's grandfather was an illegitimate son of Goethe, and this notion—ultimately dismissed by scholars—captivated Jung's imagination for some time. At the age of fourteen, Jung's mother gave him a copy of Goethe's *Faust*, and this work remained with him as a lifelong source of fascination. Jung interpreted *Faust* as an alchemical drama, portraying a process of inner transformation. Just as he chronicled his own psychological journey in *The Red Book*, Jung saw *Faust* as a symbolic record of Goethe's inner development—a life's work he completed only shortly before his death.

Thus, one can see how Jung traced his intellectual and spiritual lineage through Goethe all the way back in history through the long line of alchemists to the beginning of the Common Era. There, he found a profound connection with the Gnostics, to whom he felt a deep and enduring affinity—regarding them, like the alchemists, as ancestral spirits.

Alchemy, for Jung, served as a vital bridge between modern depth psychology and the ancient wisdom traditions. Thus, he afforded the subject central importance in his *Collected Works*. Comprising eighteen volumes, the *Collected Works* includes three volumes (12, 13, and 14) explicitly devoted to alchemy. Beyond these, numerous other volumes contain substantial references to the subject. From the moment Jung began his focused engagement with alchemy in 1928 until his death in 1961, the "golden veins" of alchemical thought ran consistently through his writings.

Indeed, nearly all of Jung's work after 1930 contains some reference to alchemy. What follows is a list of Jung's explicitly alchemical writings, including their original dates of publication and their location within the *Collected Works*:

1929 – "Commentary on 'The Secret of the Golden Flower'" (CW 13)

1936/1944 – "Individual Dream Symbolism in Relation to Alchemy" (CW 12)

1937/1944 – "Religious Ideas in Alchemy" (CW 12)

1937/1954 – "The Visions of Zosimos" (CW 13)

1942 – "Paracelsus as a Spiritual Phenomenon" (CW 13)

1943/1948 – "The Spirit Mercurius" (CW 13)

1945 – "Introduction to the Religious and Psychological Problems of Alchemy" (CW 12)

1945/1954 – "The Philosophical Tree" (CW 13)

1946 – "The Psychology of the Transference" (CW 16)

1951 – *Aion* (CW 9ii)

1955/56 – *Mysterium Coniunctionis* (CW 14)

As indicated, Jung began his alchemical studies in 1929 with his "Commentary" on *The Secret of the Golden Flower*. It took him some years to become familiar with the strange language of alchemy, which he did by creating an index of terms and expressions. He then used his acquired knowledge of alchemical processes and images to interpret a series of dreams and visions shared with him by the physicist Wolfgang Pauli. In this analysis, Jung identified a psychological process unfolding within Pauli's inner world—one that he found to be closely related to the symbolic transformations described in the alchemical literature. He first presented this material in 1936 at Eranos, and subsequently revised and incorporated it as Part II of his volume *Psychology and Alchemy*. The following year, at the 1937 Eranos Conference, he presented a paper titled "Religious Ideas in Alchemy," offering perhaps his clearest introduction to his approach to interpreting alchemical imagery through a psychological lens. This paper was later published as Part III of the same volume.

As a brief aside, the Eranos Conferences (established in 1933) were held annually on the grounds of an estate owned by Olga Fröbe-Kapteyn on the shores of Lago Maggiore, just outside Ascona, Switzerland. These gatherings brought together distinguished scholars of religion from many parts of the world.[12] Conceived as a forum for dialogue between East and West, the conferences provided a unique platform for interdisciplinary exchange. Jung, representing the field of depth psychology, was a central figure from the outset, participating regularly until 1952, when age and illness prevented his continued attendance. It was at Eranos that many of Jung's most significant papers—generally always engaging in alchemy—were first presented. Following the conferences, he would go home, rewrite the papers for publication in the *Eranos Jahrbuch*, and later expand them further for publication as chapters in his own books.

In 1937, Jung gave a lecture at Eranos titled "The Visions of Zosimos," based on a text by the fourth century alchemist Zosimos of Panopolis, generally credited with being the earliest verifiable alchemical author in the West.[13] A few years later, in 1941, Jung gave two lectures in Einsiedeln, Switzerland, titled, "Paracelsus as a Spiritual Phenomenon." Both essays were later published in revised and expanded versions, and they appear in Jung's *Collected Works*, volume thirteen*. In 1943, Jung wrote a paper titled "The Spirit Mercurius," which was also originally delivered as an Eranos lecture. Attendance at Eranos was greatly reduced during the war years, as

---

[12] For a full account, see Hans Thomas Hakl's comprehensive history, *Eranos: An Alternative Intellectual History of the Twentieth Century*.
[13] See J. Lindsay, *The Origins of Alchemy in Graeco-Roman Egypt*, 323ff.

Switzerland was isolated from the rest of Europe and only Swiss nationals could participate. Nonetheless, there was a sufficient number of Swiss scholars to sustain the conference through this period.

After the war, publication of Jung's *Collected Works* commenced under the sponsorship of the Bollingen Foundation. Originally conceived in the late 1930s by Mary and Paul Mellon, the Foundation's activities had been suspended during the war. After Mary Mellon's sudden and unexpected death in 1946, Paul Mellon continued to support the project in her memory, aiming to fulfil her greatest dream.[14] Although *Psychology and Alchemy* is designated as Volume 12 in the *Collected Works*, it was chosen as the first to be published. The editors justified this decision by stating: "It may be said that round the material contained in this volume the major portion of his later work revolves. On this account *Psychology and Alchemy* is being published first, though it is not Volume 1 of the *Collected Works*."[15] Clearly, the editors recognized the centrality of alchemy in Jung's later writings. The urgency to publish this volume was no doubt also driven by the response to the German edition, which generated considerable interest following its publication in 1946. Translator R.F.C. Hull and the editorial team were eager

---

[14] For all the interesting details, see W. McGuire, *Bollingen: An Adventure in Collecting the Past.*

[15] Jung, *Psychology and Alchemy*, vii.

to make it available to Jung's English-speaking audience, who were especially curious about its contents.

In 1945, Jung wrote a paper in honour of the botanist Gustav Senn, titled "The Philosophical Tree," in which he traced and interpreted the tree symbol in alchemy. The tree, he argued, is a symbol of the gradual manifestation in time of the Self's innate potential, thus representing the individuation process. The following year he published the quasi-clinical alchemical work *The Psychology of the Transference*, in which he employed pictures and texts from one of his favourite alchemical texts, the *Rosarium Philosophorum*. In this profound work, Jung related the alchemical process of transformation shown in the alchemical text to the therapeutic relationship. His other works on alchemy focus on archetypal themes and symbolism, rather than clinical issues, though comments on clinical work are interspersed throughout. Indeed, Jung's mind was never far from the reality of analytical practice.

Jung's final work, constituting his *magnum opus* on alchemy, was *Mysterium Coniunctionis*, published as Volume 14 of the *Collected Works*. He began drafting the text in the early 1940s, but set it aside to publish *Aion* and other works. He ultimately returned to it and brought it to completion in 1955. In the "Foreword," Jung explained that the original impetus for the work was an essay by his friend, Karl Kerényi, on the Aegean Festival scene in Goethe's *Faust, Part II*.[16] Jung initially intended to write a commentary on Kerényi's essay, but as he delved deeper into the material, he realized that the project was growing into something much larger and more significant. Eventually, it became the massive *Mysterium Coniunctionis*—a veritable summary of his years of studying the hoary texts of alchemy, focused principally on the key alchemical theme of the union of opposites.

From approximately 1935 until the end of his life in 1961, Jung was accompanied by a kind of *soror mystica* (to use the alchemical term for the alchemist's assistant), Marie-Louise von Franz.

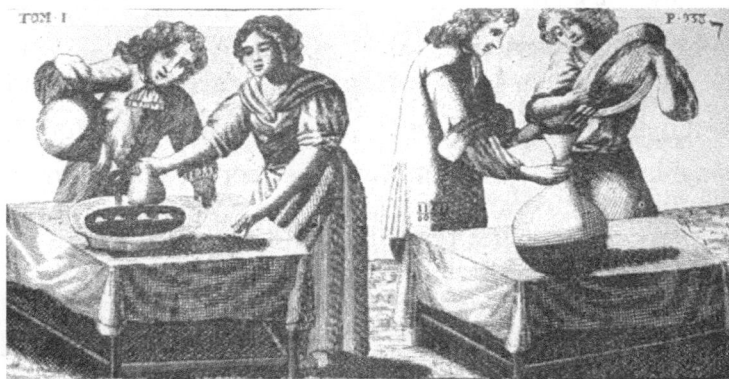

Von Franz first met Jung in the 1930s as an eighteen-year-old Gymnasium student, and soon began analysis with him while pursuing her studies at the University of

---

[16] Jung, *Mysterium Coniunctionis*, xiii.

Zurich. Being a student, she lacked the financial means to pay for analysis, so she worked for Jung in exchange for sessions. Recognized by Jung as his "little genius," von Franz went on to become a distinguished scholar in her own right, completing her doctoral dissertation on Latin interpreters of Homer's *Iliad*.[17] Her command of classical languages was extraordinary, while Jung's was sufficient but modest by comparison. I imagine the two of them in frequent conversation about the alchemy texts: "What does this passage mean?" "How do you interpret that?" "How would you translate that phrase?" When Jung's *Aion* published in 1951, the volume included an essay by von Franz titled "The Passion of Perpetua"—a psychological commentary on the dreams of the early Christian martyr. And when *Mysterium Coniunctionis* was published in German between 1955 and 1956, it appeared as a three-volume set: the first two volumes comprised Jung's magnum opus, while the third was von Franz's *Aurora Consurgens*, commenting on a medieval alchemical text traditionally attributed to Thomas Aquinas.

Conclusion

In alchemy, Jung found evidence of the archetypal basis of psychological transformation, which he called individuation. Indeed, a transformative process with a definite goal is one way of talking about the alchemical

---

[17] Von Franz, *Die aesthetischen Anschuungen der Jliasscholien*.

opus. When alchemists speak of the opus, they describe a work oriented toward something ultimate and meaningful—not endless and cyclical repetition (akin to Nietzsche's "eternal return") or aimless drifting. Rather, the stages of alchemy reach toward a goal that is definite, and Jung found in this a compelling analogue to the individuation process as he observed it in both himself and his patients.

The sense of historical continuity that Jung discovered in the works of the alchemists was not only important for him personally, but it also linked modern depth psychology to older traditions, extending as far back as the Greek philosophers and the ancient Egyptians. Jung felt that, by exploring alchemy, he was putting depth psychology on a solid footing because, as he wrote in *MDR*, you can't have depth psychology without history—or indeed, without "deep history." You can have a psychology of consciousness without history, but you can't have a *depth* psychology without history. Thus, for Jung, it was essential to create a link to the past, and he found that in alchemy. What he really wanted to do, in the final analysis, was to reunite spirit and matter and link the modern person back to an awareness of the *unus mundus*—the ultimate unity of psyche and matter.

Lecture Two
Alchemical Symbols as States of Mind

Many people stumble when they come across Jung's late writings on alchemical symbols and themes, which are densely packed with references to obscure authors and works in Latin and Greek that are likely to baffle readers lacking in a strong classical education. The alchemical texts also stymied Jung when he first tried to read them. He found them utterly impenetrable, a confabulation of mumbo-jumbo. While his own writing on this esoteric subject is not quite as densely opaque as the sources he studied, it remains difficult for modern readers, even those who are relatively well educated by contemporary standards. To gain entry into this forested material, therefore, one needs to practice patience, similar to what Jung and the alchemists themselves must have done as they puzzled over the ancient texts and arcane procedures. Jung's late works on psychology and alchemy, which appear in the *Collected Works* volumes 9ii, 12, 13 and 14, are rich and profound, and I consider them representative of the best of his thought in his mature and late periods of life. But they are not easy reads.

When Jung set out to study alchemy seriously, he created an index in which he noted the locations of terms and concepts that were repeated in the texts he had sourced from bookstores and libraries. From this index, he was able to create a personal lexicon to help him make sense of the otherwise nearly indecipherable writings. "I noticed," he wrote in *MDR*, "that certain strange expressions and turns of phrase were frequently repeated. For example, '*solve et coagula*,' '*unum vas*,' '*lapis*,' '*prima materia*,' '*Mercurius*,' etc."[18] In time, these terms would become as familiar to him as the vocabulary he used in his other psychological writings. Likewise, for readers of Jung's alchemical writings, these terms resonate as familiar symbols.

In this chapter, I will cover some of the key terms that Jung discusses throughout his works, in the hope that this will aid readers in navigating Jung's writings on alchemy and gaining at least a preliminary understanding of the messages he sought to convey.

Part III of *Psychology and Alchemy* (*Collected Works* vol. 12), "Religious Ideas in Alchemy," is a good place to begin. This piece of writing started out as a lecture at the Eranos Conference in 1936, with the title "*Die*

---

[18] Jung, *Memories, Dreams, Reflections*, 205.

Erlösungsvorstellungen in der Alchemie."[19] The same title is retained in the German *Gesammelte Werke,* but it has been changed in the English translation ("religious ideas" is not a translation of *Erlösungsvorstellungen,* which actually means "salvation concepts" and implies redemption and liberation). In his Eranos lecture, Jung argued that the alchemical authors claimed that their procedures could lead to the salvation of the soul—a claim that brought them into direct conflict with Church theologians. The operations of alchemy, they argued, were positioned on the same footing as the rituals of the Church. However, what the Church offered in baptism, confession, the rite of the Mass, and so forth, the alchemists could not do with their methods because they lacked the means of grace given by God through the sacrifice of his Son, Jesus Christ.

"Religious Ideas in Alchemy" opens with a picture depicting "the principal symbols of alchemy."[20]

---

[19] The theme of the Eranos conference in 1936 was *"Gestaltung der Erlösungsidee in Ost und West"* ("Forms of the Salvation Idea, East and West"). Two lectures given that year, "Angst und Erlösung im Protestantismus" by Paul Tillich and "Die Erlösungsidee im Judentum" by Heinz Westman, were not included in the *Eranos Jahrbuch* because German authorities objected to these two speakers—the first a critic of National Socialism and the second a Jew. The inclusion of these authors would have put the distribution of the *Jahrbuch* in Germany at risk. Their essays were later published by the Eranos Foundation in 1986.

[20] Jung, *Psychology and Alchemy*, para. 224.

Trismosin, *La Toyson d'or* (1612)

The Latin text in the circle surrounding the symbols reads: *Invenies ocultu lapidem visita interiora terrae rectificando* ("You will find the hidden stone by visiting the interior of the earth"). This "hidden stone" is the mystical *lapis philosophorum*—the quintessential alchemical symbol of the soul's ultimate true nature—and "the interior of the earth" is the collective unconscious. This is the secret of alchemy. Liberation requires a journey to the interior. In response to this symbol, Jung quoted a familiar sentence by the alchemist Johann Daniel Mylius (1583–1642): "*Habentibus symbolum facilis est transitus*" ("For those who have the symbol the passage is easy").[21]

The first four chapters in Part III of *Psychology and Alchemy*—"Basic Concepts of Alchemy," "The Psychic Nature of the Alchemical Work," "The Work," and "The Prima Materia"—form an excellent and exceptionally readable introduction to some of the basic terms and concepts of alchemy. They begin with a comment on the history of alchemy: "Slowly, in the course of the eighteenth century, alchemy perished in its own obscurity. Its method of explanation... was incompatible with the spirit of the enlightenment and particularly with the dawning science of chemistry."[22] Recall, however, that in his dream, Jung found himself trapped in the seventeenth century.[23] Indeed, his alchemical writings reach back in history, bringing his readers into contact with the pre-Enlightenment mentality of classical alchemy.

It is important to understand that, in his articles and books on alchemy, Jung was not writing a history of science. It was not his intention to present an objective account of alchemy as a predecessor to the science of chemistry. That project could be left to other scholars. Rather, his purpose was to discover the parallels between the symbolic productions of the modern psyche and the

---

[21] Ibid., para 225.
[22] Ibid., para. 332.
[23] Jung, *Memories, Dreams, Reflections*, 203–204.

symbolic thought of the alchemists, for whom the mind-matter split was not operative. Jung was particularly interested in the mentality of the alchemists, which allowed them to explore the recesses of the unconscious more deeply than modern mentality allows. Thus, by studying the symbolic productions of the alchemists, he aimed to extend the modern understanding of the unconscious. What the alchemists described in their texts were the states of mind they saw reflected in the materials contained in their retorts and furnaces. Jung found similar patterns and images in the dreams and fantasies of his patients.

The Alchemical *Vas*

An often-repeated term in the alchemical texts is *vas*, representing the vessel or container for the process. The *vas* appears in a variety of shapes and sizes, as shown in the figure below.

The *vas*, wrote Jung, "is a kind of matrix or uterus from which the *filius philosophorum*, the miraculous stone, is to be born."[24] Its round shape mirrors "the spherical cosmos, so that the influence of the stars may contribute to the success of the operation."[25] In a footnote, Jung quoted a passage from Gerhard Dorn: "Our vessel must be such that in it matter can be influenced by the heavenly bodies. For the invisible celestial influences and the impressions of the stars are necessary to the work."[26]

The psychological translation of this statement is that, for transformation to succeed, the mind must be open to archetypal influences from the collective unconscious ("heavenly bodies"). Analysts sometimes speak of the analytic container as a *vas bene clausum*, or well-sealed vessel, to indicate its privacy and confidentiality as a free and sheltered space. At the same time, it is permeable to unconscious processes. This analytic *vas* is formed through the attitude of the analytical couple, who are both contained within the relationship and open to archetypal input from the inner constellations of stars. These manifestations from the unconscious enter the *vas* as dreams, images, and synchronistic events. Thus, the *vas* can be thought of as a "field" that is both closed off from the outer world (i.e., a sealed container protected by confidentiality) and open to the depths of the psyche that are activated in the course of the work.

---

[24] Ibid., para. 338.
[25] Ibid.
[26] Ibid., n. 17.

Prima Materia

"The basis of the *opus*, the *prima materia*, is one of the most famous secrets of alchemy."[27] This substance can be thought of as the ground of everything psychic and material, out of which everything that exists originates. In Jung's Gnostic vision, "The Seven Sermons to the Dead," as spoken by the teacher Philemon in *The Red Book*, it is called the *pleroma*—a Gnostic term for the original matrix. In psychological terms, the *prima materia* represents a state of pre-conscious wholeness, or the Self in its earliest state—one of non-differentiation. At first, it is a *massa confusa*—a mixture of the totality of psychic elements prior to their organization into oppositional pairs. Later in the course of development, the *prima materia* can be thought of as the source of the impulses, thoughts, memories, images, and so forth that fill our half-conscious minds with the flotsam and jetsam of the everyday. The alchemists assembled a collection of materials thought to contain specimens of the *prima materia*, and placed it in the *vas* for processing.

Alchemical recipes list the materials necessary for beginning the *opus*. While these ingredients may be taken literally by the adept, they also have symbolic meaning. They must be gathered carefully—from gardens, forests, junk piles, the streets—to begin the process that will eventually extract the precious *arcanum*, a mysterious substance sought from the depths of the material world.

---

[27] Ibid., para. 425.

Recipes for the *opus* were guardedly passed down through generations of alchemists by word of mouth, and sometimes recorded in books.

In *Mysterium Coniunctionis*, Jung quoted one such recipe, offering pages of interpretation on the various ingredients: "The mixture of the new heaven, of honey, Chelidonia, rosemary flowers, Mercurialis, of the red lily and human blood, with the heaven of the red or white wine or of Tartarus."[28] He concluded that the purpose of the alchemical process "was to create, in the form of a substance, that 'truth,' the celestial balsam or life principle, which is identical with the God-image. Psychologically, it was a representation of the individuation process by means of chemical substances and procedures."[29]

From a psychological perspective, the *prima materia* is a mass of mental contents in a state of chaos and disarray. It evokes the *tehom* ("the deep)" at the beginning of creation, over which the spirit of the Lord moves in the first verses of Genesis (Genesis 1:1-2). It is "without form and void," pre-psychological, and existing prior to the configuration of patterns and identities. This void state of mind is sometimes associated with the astrological and mythic figure of Saturn,[30] evoking the depressed condition that prevails at the beginning of the opus. The *prima materia* might therefore manifest as depressive thoughts, feelings, and impulses that create a

---

[28] Jung, *Mysterium Coniunctionis*, para. 683.
[29] Ibid., para. 705.
[30] Jung, "The Spirit Mercurius," *CW* 13, para. 274.

mental state of confusion and disorientation. Often, this mixture of thoughts and feelings has its roots in negative experiences (traumas), complexes, and archetypal images that exert an unconscious influence on an individual prior to entering analysis. Such material weighs heavily on consciousness, like lead—Saturn's metal.

As far as psychotherapy is concerned, the *prima materia* is hidden within the *massa confusa* of an unreflected mind, where it is mixed up and disordered but nevertheless subtly present in the clutter of everyday life—in relationships, at work, in ruminations, in dreams, and in fantasies. This "clutter" must be carefully collected and put into the *vas* of analysis. Surprisingly, it contains hidden within it the essence of the personality, which must be drawn out through careful distillation and differentiation over the course of a long analytic process. This is the art of the psychotherapeutic *opus*.

One is reminded by the alchemists that it is important to gather all of this material, no matter how lowly or unpromising it appears at first sight. After all, the arcanum is hidden in the substances that "the builders rejected" (Psalm 118:22). The analyst must receive whatever comes from the client and place it in the vessel. Nothing is too ugly or unpromising. The *prima materia* is in the welter of life experience. If some bits and pieces are left out, the desired extraction of the *arcanum* (the Self) is possible. Analysis must be like a strong stomach that can digest almost anything.

Stages of the *Opus—Nigredo, Albedo, Rubedo*

The alchemical *opus* typically unfolds across three stages (though sometimes four), and these are coded in color. Three Latin words relate to the progressive stages of the work: *nigredo*, *albedo*, and *rubedo*. The *nigredo* refers to a time of darkness—a state of mind associated with depression and confusion, just as a substance in the dark holds little energy. Sometimes this stage is represented by an image of chaos. However, it is the state of mind in which transformation of the psyche, from less to more conscious, begins.

People often enter analysis following a crisis that plunged them into a state of confusion and disorientation. This is the starting point. And it is necessary, if the process is to be at all deep. However, if an analysand is not confused when they

Figure 162. The unfettered opposites in chaos. "Chaos" is one of the names for the *nigredo*. Marolles, *Tableaux du temple des muses* (1655).[31]

---

[31] Ibid., para. 318.

begin the work, they will soon enough find themselves disoriented as the analysis deepens. Jung once said (I think in jest!): "Bring me a sane man and I will cure him." The alchemists rejoiced when the material in the *vas* turned black, as this was a sign that the transformation was beginning. Why? Because old structures must be deconstructed to make room for the new. This stage in analysis, which Jung called "confession,"[32] brings the shadow into the foreground—a necessary condition for deeper work.

The *nigredo* is followed, after a time (often a long time!), by the *albedo,* or "whitening," during which the ingredients in the vessel turn from black to white. Once the old material has been burned to a crisp, the ashes begin to turn white. This represents the beginning of a new stage—one that, for the alchemist, was associated with the dawn. At the moment of first light, darkness slowly gives way to soft glimmers of sun rays, and it becomes possible to look around and see one's surroundings. The *Aurora Consurgens* ("dawn rising"), an alchemy text attributed to Thomas Aquinas that Marie-Louise von Franz interpreted, explicates this stage of the *opus* in great detail.[33]

Psychologically, the *albedo* is associated with a state of mind that has achieved insight after a period

---

[32] Jung, "Problems of Modern Psychotherapy," *CW* 16, para. 123ff.
[33] Von Franz, *Aurora Consurgens.*

of depression and guilt, facilitated by confession. As Nietzsche wrote: "The bad conscience is an illness, there is no doubt about that, but an illness as pregnancy is an illness."[34] The *albedo* is the birth from this pregnancy of a new sense of self, based on an awareness of the shadow dynamics at play behind the screen of egocentrism. Things that were once hidden away from consciousness, whether due to repression or fear or denial, now emerge into view as a new day's light. Now, one can begin to sort out the jumble of feelings, of formerly hidden impulses and desires, and of shameful motivations that previously swam like fish in the waters of the unconscious. At this stage, one begins to develop a more realistic picture of the inner world and what is there.

Perhaps this also includes seeing through a personal or cultural complex and getting a glimpse of something deeper and broader in significance. With the birth of a sense of meaning in one's personal destiny, the stage of the *rubedo* makes its appearance. The *rubedo* refers to the rising of the sun, which brilliantly reddens the sky, bestowing not only light, but also warmth. The appearance of the *rubedo* in the *vas* warmed the heart of the alchemist, indicating that the *opus* was nearing completion. Soon, the alchemical gold would appear and the work would be complete. This was a moment to celebrate. Psychologically, the *rubedo* represents a state

---

[34] Nietzsche, *On the Genealogy of Morals*, 88.

of mind that is not only enlightened, but also energized and strong, able to act.

The *opus* thus proceeds from the darkness of unconsciousness to the dawn of consciousness and eventually a new day of energy and meaningful action. Following this, one is able to create warmth in the environment and provide what is needed for the world around them to blossom and flourish. This is the goal of the alchemical *opus*—to arrive at the state of mind represented by the *rubedo*.

Aqua Permanens

A frequently used alchemical phrase is *aqua permanens*, meaning the "eternal water" or "water of life." This phrase references the words of Jesus: "Anyone who drinks this water will soon become thirsty again. But those who drink the water I give will never be thirsty again. It becomes a fresh, bubbling spring within them, giving them eternal life."[35]

The alchemists considered the *aqua permanens* a solvent with mystical properties, related to Mercurius (mercury), the metallic liquid and agent of transformation. Woven into Jung's texts as a constant motif, it can be understood as an equivalent to the *lapis philosoporum*, even though they seem very different to the literal mind—

---

[35] John 4:13.

one a stone and the other water, one solid and the other liquid. The alchemical mind loved paradox, as Jung emphasized in a chapter in *Mysterium Coniunctionis* titled "The Paradoxa." Thus, when engaging with alchemy, the rational mind must learn to adjust. Basically, we can understand *aqua permanens* as a transformative agent that washes and transforms common everyday thoughts and feelings into noble ones.

Aqua permanens is necessary for uniting the opposites in alchemy. In fact, it is the very medium in which union takes place. One finds it in the Mercurial Fountain at the beginning of the *Rosarium Philosophorum* and the subsequent bath into which *Sol* and *Luna* (King and Queen) enter naked and there unite. Jung described this alchemical process of union in his essay "On the Psychology of the Transference," and the entire *Mysterium Coniunctionis* is "an inquiry into the separation and synthesis of psychic opposites in alchemy" (the volume's subtitle). The *aqua permanens* may also be considered a metaphor for the "field" created by the analytic relationship, wherein two psyches unite and become one in a transcendent third.

Salt, Sulfur, Mercury

The alchemists worked primarily with three materials: salt, sulfur, and mercury. The alchemists' salt, as they wrote, was not table salt but a complex symbolic substance.

It was "a synonym for the *albedo*, and is identical with 'the white stone, the white sun, the full moon, the fruitful white earth, cleansed and calcined'....one of its principal meanings is *soul*...it is the 'white woman' a spark of the *anima mundi*."[36] With its white color, it was designated feminine and used as such in the alchemical operations involving *coniunctio* or union.

Salt also evokes emotional suffering (think of the salt in one's tears), as well as the wisdom that comes from suffering—assuming it does not turn into bitterness. James Hillman wrote an essay on this aspect of the salt symbol, titled "The Suffering of Salt." In this work, he claimed that Jung examined "salt in a scholarly manner in order to gain an objective meaning of this alchemical substance. I am attempting to bring over to the reader its substantiality as a commonly recognized experience."[37] On his part, Jung touched on this experience of salt as suffering, but he also reflected more broadly and philosophically on salt as "a cosmic principle...correlated with the feminine, lunar side and with the upper, light half [of the quaternity]" and "one of the many designations for the arcane substance."[38] Basically, salt symbolizes a cool and receptive attitude. Jung wrote: "It [i.e., salt] represents the feminine principle of Eros, which brings

---

[36] Jung, *Mysterium Coniunctionis*, paras. 320–21.
[37] Hillman, "The Suffering of Salt," 55.
[38] Jung, *Mysterium Coniunctionis*, para. 240.

everything into relationship, in an almost perfect way."[39] As a state of consciousness, salt is receptive, close to the emotions, and relational; as a mood, it can be like those petulant, bitter, and withdrawn moments that take over consciousness episodically.

Sulfur, in contrast, is dynamic energy that is red in color and represented by *Sol* (the Sun). In processes involving *coniunctio* (union or synthesis), sulfur is the masculine energy engaged with salt as the feminine. It is the aggressive element: "Its fiery nature is unanimously stressed."[40] Like salt, sulfur can be positive or negative; it is duplex. It can be burning and corrosive, or it can be golden and mild, like the sun. When *Sol* and *Luna* (the Moon) interact, according to Paracelsus, they produce a child, Mercurius.[41] Sulfur is also, like salt, a spiritual substance—"the soul not only of the metals but of all living things."[42] As a state of consciousness, it is fiery and assertive; and as an attitude or mood, it is argumentative and opinionated.

Mercury is a strange metal because it is normally liquid and not solid. Named *Mercurius duplex* by the alchemists, the material fascinated them, and they used it as a magical agent that could dissolve (*salve*) and coagulate (*coagula*) materials and, in so doing, bring

---

[39] Ibid., para. 322.
[40] Ibid., para. 134.
[41] Ibid., para. 135.
[42] Ibid., para. 156.

new products into being. In their texts, they depicted Mercurius as androgenous and holding a magic wand that he used to induce transformations in the alchemical *vas*.

As the necessary catalyst, Mercurius is present at the beginning and throughout the alchemical process, bringing about transformation in the alchemical interaction between salt and sulfur before disappearing from the process. Moreover, Mercurius is regarded as a trickster—somewhat unstable and not always reliable, and prone to creating chaos and mischief. The adjective "mercurial" derives from this name. Sometimes, Mercurius creates disruptions and trouble, and sometimes he is the helpful guiding spirit. Jung wrote a long essay about this fascinating figure and identified him as the "spirit of the unconscious."[43] Thus, psychologically speaking, he personifies the dynamic aspect of the Self. As a state of mind, he is shifty.

The *Opus*

Importantly, alchemy was an *opus* (Lat. for "work"). It did not happen spontaneously on its own. Adepts had to study and sweat, as we can see in the pictures of their laboratories.

---

[43] See Jung, "The Spirit Mercurius," *CW* 13.

The project had to be engaged in deliberately, arduously, and with great dedication. Likewise, Jung sometimes wrote of individuation as an *opus*, especially in his discussion of analysis.

On the one hand, individuation is a natural process of development that runs its course without conscious assistance. In that sense, it is not an *opus* but a type of growth that occurs in both the psyche and the physical body, culminating in its full stature. As an *opus*, however, individuation is worked on consciously by the ego, in cooperation with the unconscious and the inherent energies of the psyche. The alchemical expression *Deo concedente* ("God conceding, God willing") implies both synchronicity and magical blessings, as well as labor, suffering, and hard work. In Jung's most important and interesting writing on the application of alchemy to individuation, he frequently employed two terms: *meditatio* and *imaginatio*, meaning meditation and imagination. What did Jung mean by these terms? And what about the alchemist? I only mention them here in passing and will consider them more deeply later.

Here is a classic symbol of the *opus*.

It is called the *Trimurti* picture. "The triangle symbolizes the tendency of the universe to converge towards the point of unity," Jung wrote.

> The tortoise represents Vishnu; the lotus growing out of the skull between two flames, Shiva. The shining sun of Brahma forms the background. The whole picture corresponds to the alchemical *opus*, the tortoise symbolizing the *massa confusa*, the skull the *vas* of transformation, and the flower the 'self' or wholeness.[44]

---

[44] Jung, *Psychology and Alchemy*, para. 199.

The alchemist saw the skull—the home of consciousness or the mind—as the place of transformation, or the alchemical *vas*. In this image, the flower blossoming out of the skull is the result of the process of transformation.

Solve et Coagula

The phrase *solve et coagula* ("dissolve and coagulate") refers to an operation in the alchemical *opus* whereby the material in the alchemical *vas* is dissolved and turned into a liquid, before coagulating into something solid. The process resembles that of a wound: first it bleeds, then the blood coagulates and eventually ceases to flow. In alchemy, this process is repeated many times. Dissolving is performed through the application of water, and coagulation is done through the application of earth. Water dissolves what is hardened and rigid, or what has been formed and shaped but needs to be transformed; earth solidifies the liquid and "grounds" it.

In psychoanalysis, we speak of complexes as being hard and rigid, repeating their fixed patterns in perpetuity. These need to be dissolved through the waters of analysis. But how is this done? Sometimes we require the application of stringent or astringent liquids to dissolve a complex; sometimes love does the trick; sometimes compassion; sometimes anger. In any case, there is a breakthrough, and the complex is taken apart and dissolved. Moving into the coagulation means making the dissolved substance solid—something to stand on or hold onto that doesn't float around, like a fundamental value. Coagulation brings some ground under the feet, enabling one to take a position, to take a stand. For this, earth is needed.

Circulatio

Circulatio represents the circulation of the process. It gives one hope in the spiral movement—that the direction is going toward something better and not just a repetition. However, sometimes it must circulate through the alchemical *vas* from bottom to top and back down again, over and over throughout the process. This is all part of the distillation, or brewing process, aimed at refinement through the circulation, making the arcana more conscious. The *transformatio*, meaning transformation, is what the whole *opus* is about. Transformation is not the same as change, as in changing from one thing to another. Rather, transformation means drawing something out of what was there all along, bringing it to consciousness, and giving it more expression. It is about moving possibilities, dynamics, and energies from the unconscious side of potential into consciousness. In this process, a structure forms, and a new identity and personality takes shape. This transformation, moving from potential to actualization, is the movement from the *prima materia* to the *lapis*, or what the alchemists called "our gold"—a spiritual substance of permanent value.

Lithos ou lithos

Lithos ou lithos is a Greek phrase meaning "the stone that is not a stone," referring to a "stone" (i.e., the lapis) that is not material, but psychological and spiritual. It is an attitude—a state of mind. This phrase underscores the symbolic nature of alchemy: it is not only, or even principally, about turning material lead into gold. As Jung wrote: "The alchemical opus deals in the main not just with chemical experiments as such, but with something resembling psychic processes expressed in pseudo-chemical language."[45] The materials that were brought into the alchemist's laboratory and the processes described are metaphors for psychological conditions and processes. The phrase *lithos ou lithos*, also spoken of as "our gold," shows the alchemists' awareness that they were producing something in the psychic, rather than the physical, laboratory. "Our gold" is the psychic stone, representing a spiritual achievement and acquisition. This "stone" is said to possess healing properties and the capacity to transform other substances—an apt metaphor for the transformative influence exerted by individuals who have gone through the alchemical process of psychological integration.

In the following photograph, Jung appears as an old alchemist at Bollingen, pipe in mouth (as always), working on his stone. However, the image captures

---

[45] Jung, *CW* 12, para. 342.

more than a simple act of craftsmanship, showing Jung actively working on his own individuation. The stone he is carving—what he would later call the "orphan stone"—was part of a larger symbolic endeavor. For Jung, Bollingen represented the Self: a symbolic house that he constructed by hand over many years. This project embodied the spirit of the alchemist in Jung as he worked on himself in various ways. *The Red Book* represents one phase of this long inner work, encapsulating his midlife transformation. His building of the tower at Bollingen marked a later phase, serving as another expression of individuation. At Bollingen, inner and outer dimensions of the psyche coalesced in the form of artistic creations, functioning as a tangible extension of his inner work.

Lecture Three
Alchemy as Active Imagination

In his writings, Jung argued that alchemy was a predecessor of depth psychology, as the alchemists made use of the technique he called "active imagination." While they were certainly busy with recipes, flasks, vessels, and furnaces, they were also (and perhaps more fundamentally) engaged in an inner process of psychological and spiritual transformation. Jung was particularly interested in this aspect of their work—what was going on in the alchemists' subjectivity while engaging in the *opus*. To examine this dynamic, Jung applied the psychological concept of projection, arguing that the alchemical *opus* was simultaneously subjective and objective—psychological and material. Although the *opus* included physical experimentation in the laboratory, Jung saw in the alchemy texts a symbolic expression of psychic processes encoded in pseudo-chemical language. The alchemists, in his view, experienced their work on two levels: as material operations that could be objectively perceived, and as reflections of their own psyches in transformation.

Jung maintained that the alchemical process was fundamentally a psychic process projected onto the material substances contained within the alchemical *vas*. Indeed, what we often interpret as objective perception is, in many cases, a fusion of external stimuli and internal imagery. We may believe we are observing something "out there," when in fact we are projecting our inner content onto the external form, filling in the details with a story. For example, we may think we see something on the wall. It moves, then it changes, and maybe it even speaks to us. But what we are really doing is speaking to *ourselves*, seeing *ourselves* in a mirror but not recognizing that reality. We have all experienced such projections. If you lie down in the grass on a summer's day and stare into the sky, you may see some clouds moving about. Then suddenly you may see a horse, a cow, a dog, or a cat. You may be aware that the image is not in the clouds at all, but even still, it can be strong and convincing, and if you are psychologically naïve you may believe that you are perceiving, rather than projecting. The message you receive from the cloud-dog will be convincing, and you may take it as true communication from the beyond. But a psychologist would say that you are seeing something that's taking place in the background of your own mind. Now, if you really concentrate on that inner process and pursue it, you will be doing what the alchemists were doing in their experiments: observing and following the images projected onto the *prima materia* cooking in the flask.

In the darkness of the material world—which was scientifically opaque to the alchemists in ways it is not to us today—the alchemists unknowingly discovered the interior world of the psyche. To recognize this as an inner, rather than an outer, space would have constituted a tremendous advance in consciousness—one that did not occur until centuries later, well after the alchemists closed shop. Such a realization would have meant coming to the point of understanding, or at least being able to consider, that the drama unfolding before them was subjective in nature, laden with meaning for their personal lives. Some of the later alchemical writers, such as Gerhard Dorn, had a glimpse of this understanding, thinking more as philosophers than as experimenters in a chemical laboratory. For the medieval alchemists, however, the drama remained an external process, interpreted cosmologically, rather than psychologically. They believed the *opus* aimed at the redemption of the hidden soul of the world, the *anima mundi*.

In their vessels, the alchemist saw images and gave them names, just as the astrologers named the planets and stars. These acts of naming were also processes of interpretation, rooted in the symbolic tradition. For instance, the appearance of certain shifting forms in the substance might be identified as Mercurius, as in the image below.

What the alchemists actually saw in the vessel is unclear. However, in rendering these visions through painting, they interpreted them according to unconscious expectations, using apperception, rather than objective perception. In the above image, for example, the flame below the vessel likely reflects the physical reality of the laboratory set-up, while within the well-sealed *vas*, a winged figure is half-submerged in a bath. This figure is identified as Mercurius, the agent of transformation in the alchemical *opus*.

For the alchemists, such vivid visions held profound significance—at times even surpassing the authority of Holy Scripture. This was a bold and potentially dangerous claim in the context of the Middle Ages, when the Bible was revered as the literal Word of God and deviation from orthodoxy could result in charges of heresy, leading to execution by burning at the stake. Nonetheless, some alchemists believed that the revelations received through their laboratory experiences carried truths equivalent to, or even greater than, those found in sacred texts. In fact, some went so far as to compare the transformations they witnessed in the laboratory to the transubstantiation mystery in the Mass.

How was this possible, given the religious and philosophical understanding of the time? The alchemists concluded that the *opus* must have been divinely ordained. The alchemical text *Novum lumen* affirms this perspective.

> To cause things hidden in the shadow to appear, and to take away the shadow from them, this is permitted to the intelligent philosopher by God through nature...All these things happen, and the eyes of the common men do not see them, but the eyes of the understanding [*intellectus*] and of the imagination perceive them [*percipient*] with true and truest vision [*visu*].[46]

The visions that revealed themselves to the alchemists were understood as "unveilings"—removals of the shadows concealing the truths captured in nature. In other

---

[46] Quoted in Jung, *CW* 12, para. 350.

words, they were "revelations," akin to those found in sacred scripture.

The Apocalypse of John represents one such book of revelation in the Bible. "Apocalypse" means, literally, taking off the veil and revealing what has been hidden behind it. Just as God revealed divine mysteries to John, so too was it believed that God had endowed the philosopher (i.e., the alchemist) with the capacity to uncover the divine mystery in nature. Central to this worldview was belief in the *anima mundi*, or soul of the world, which was thought to be a piece of the Divinity left behind in creation. While revealed theology drew on scripture as its authority, natural philosophy was based on revelations discerned in the natural world. Through careful observation, the alchemist was thought capable of perceiving the face and mind of God within creation. What remained hidden in the shadow of matter would, through divine permission and philosophical insight, step forward into the light. The common person could not see this, but the trained eyes and imagination of the alchemist could perceive it with "true and truest vision."

The combination of imagination plus intellect was considered a God-given faculty for uncovering the divine yet hidden *anima mundi*. This belief rested on the premise that God's creation was itself a form of revelation, though not immediately apparent to the ordinary observer. The image of the Creator was seen as veiled by the opacity of material substance. However, through meditative reflection and imagination, one could catch glimpses of the divine light. Jung later appropriated this idea, stripping away its metaphysical and theological layers and arguing that what was actually being intuited in such visionary states was something of the highest psychological value—the Self, residing in the archetypal depths of the collective unconscious. In analytical practice, we sometimes replicate this visioning process through the method of active imagination.

Alchemists used the term *vera imaginatio* ("true imagination") and drew a distinction between this type of imagination—a visionary capacity capable of disclosing another reality—and vain fantasy. Jung was fascinated by this idea, recognizing a parallel to his own experience of active imagination while creating *The Red Book*. Using active imagination, he witnessed scenes and images, encountered imaginal figures with whom he could converse, and experienced episodes of a magical and supernatural order. All the while, he was conscious, maintaining an intact ego, identity, and reality. He understood that the figures he encountered were not *symbols* of the inner realities of the unconscious, but fundamental aspects of himself, conveying core truths, archetypal patterns, and essential elements and processes of his psychic nature. For Jung, the *vera imaginatio* was a means of revelation that ultimately led to an experience of the Self, and he viewed this as fundamentally analogous to the inner journey undertaken by the alchemists in their labours.

In *Psychology and Alchemy*, Jung quoted an anonymous author: "I pray you, look with the eyes of the mind at this little tree of the grain of wheat, regarding all its circumstances, that you may be able to plant the tree of the philosophers."[47] This clearly indicates the use of active imagination in the *opus*—a work in which the alchemists perceived not only with their physical senses, but also "the eyes of the mind." While the alchemists mixed metals and chemicals and carefully observed what was transpiring in the *vas,* they also engaged in a mode of inner vision, using their mind's eye to observe "the little tree of the grain of wheat" and watch it develop.

In contrast, the process of modern chemistry is entirely objective. While a scientist may observe some subjective reactions to the experiment, these are not considered relevant to the integrity of the process. The outcome of the chemical process is presumed independent of the scientist's mind. Not so in alchemy. In the alchemical tradition, the *opus* depends on the alchemist's observations of the images in the *vas*. The observer and the process are one. The *opus* cannot proceed without the observer, who looks with the eyes of the mind. This link between the subjective and the objective is the essential condition of the alchemical process.

From one of his favourite alchemical texts, the *Rosarium philosophorum*, Jung quoted: "Who therefore

---

[47] Ibid., para. 357.

knows the salt and its solution knows the hidden secret of the wise men of old. Therefore, turn your mind upon the salt and think not of other things, for in it alone [i.e., the mind] is the science concealed and the most excellent and most hidden secret of all the ancient philosophers."[48] The Latin text uses the phrase "*in ipsa sola,*" and Jung questioned whether it is the *salt* that is to be observed or the mind, because the words are "close cousins."[49] Indeed, there is an identity between the salt in the vessel and the mind of the alchemist. According to Khunrath, the salt is not only the physical center of the earth, but at the same time, the *sal sapientiae* ("salt of wisdom").

Wisdom does not belong to the salt that you put on your potatoes! Rather, when we say "the salt of wisdom," we are referring to a quality of mind. Khunrath instructed the alchemists to direct their feelings, senses, reasoning, and thoughts to this salt alone. Elsewhere, the anonymous author of the *Rosarium Philosophorum* wrote that the work must be performed "with true and not with fantastic imagination," and that the stone can only be found "when the search lies heavy on the searcher."[50] Thus, the burden of the *opus* fell on the alchemist. The alchemist was the locus of the work, and the alchemist's mind was where the operations took place.

---

[48] Ibid., para. 359.
[49] Ibid., para. 360.
[50] Ibid.

Cultivating the mind includes study, and the alchemists placed great value on work in the library, reading books and papers pertaining to theory and the operations conducted in the laboratory. The intellect played an essential role in their chemical and spiritual endeavours, and it was believed that rigorous study would have the effect of activating psychological processes in the adept. Such intense engagement in study no doubt affected the alchemists' psychic lives, as it does ours, today. Deep reading takes the reader into the thoughts of the author, and this inevitably stirs the psyche in its deeper layers, soften constellating symbols in later dreams. Jung quoted an alchemy text by Richardus Angelicus, a thirteenth-century Canon at St. Paul's Cathedral in London: "Therefore all those who desire to attain the blessing of this art should apply themselves to study, should gather the truth from the books and not from invented fables and untruthful works. There is no way by which this art can truly be found (although men meet with many deceptions), except by completing their studies and understanding the words of the philosophers."[51] Here, again, we see a critical distinction being made between the true and the false: some works guide the mind to truth, while others are fables that lead the mind astray. The alchemical canon functioned as a kind of philosophical scripture, and the alchemist—like the theologian—was

---

[51] Ibid., para. 362.

expected to approach these texts with both intellectual discipline and spiritual openness.

Meditatio and *Imaginatio*—Two Types of Active Imagination

Jung viewed alchemy as a primarily introverted undertaking. This is because the alchemists, while working with material objects in the laboratory, were simultaneously engaged in the introverted activities of *meditatio* and *imaginatio*. Alchemy, in this sense, could be understood as an extended meditation. The *opus* often spanned many years, and in an age of shorter life expectancy, could easily occupy the better part of an alchemist's life.

A long meditation involves sustained observation and interaction with what emerges in the material being observed. In analysis, the *meditatio* focuses on dreams, fantasies, active imagination, memories, thoughts, and whatever else appears in the life of the analysand. Some of these elements are elusive and subtle, including dreams. On this point, Jung described: "The tendency to run away…is attributed not to the operator but to the transforming substance. Mercurius is evasive and is labelled *servus* (servant) or *cervus fugitivus* (fugitive stag)."[52] So easily, a thought or an image can escape from consciousness and fall back into the darkness of the psychic forest. Eirenaeus Philalethes says of the

---

[52] Ibid., para. 187.

servus: "You must be very wary how you lead him, for if he can find an opportunity he will give you the slip, and leave you in a world of misfortune."[53] Who hasn't had this experience of the fugitive stag? You wake up in the morning and say, "My God! I had an amazing dream last night, but where is it, where did it go?" It slips away. The spotlight here is placed not so much on the ability or inability of the ego to hold attention, but on what it is observing that gives the slip. Mercurius is a trickster and a very slippery character indeed.

The alchemical *meditatio*, however, is more than mere reflection; it is a form of inner dialogue. Ruland's *Lexicon alchemiae* defines it as follows: "The word meditatio is used when a man has an inner dialogue with someone unseen. It may be with God, when He is invoked, or with himself, or with his good angel."[54] The below image depicts two angels on either side of a meditating alchemist—presumably a good angel on the right and a bad angel on the left. The alchemist is the site of encounter with these inner forces, manifesting as opposing aspects of his shadow.

Anyone who has engaged effectively with active imagination is familiar with this inner dialogue. It is an essential part of the confrontation with the unconscious. Ruland's definition states clearly that when the alchemical

---

[53] Ibid.
[54] Ibid., para. 390.

texts describe meditation, they are not referring to mere cogitation or reflection, akin to rumination. Rather, they are pointing to an explicitly inner dialogue. This implies a live relationship with the answering voice of "the other" in ourselves—the unconscious. As Jung wrote, this is a pivot point in the *opus*.

The Red Book is replete with such dialogues with imaginal figures. We see Jung dialoguing with Soul, Elijah, Salome, Philemon, Izdubar, and others. Some twenty figures come alive in the active imaginations recorded in this text. The alchemical *meditation* features centrally in these inner dialogues. There is, for instance, an interesting and rather long and difficult dialogue with Philemon about the nature and practice of magic.[55] The

---

[55] Jung, *The Red Book*: *Liber Secundus*, Chapter 21.

narrator asks Philemon to explain magic to him, but Philemon resists. He attempts to trick an answer out of Philemon. Then Philemon tricks him back. The point is that he is a real and active figure who speaks back to Jung, the meditator. The imaginal figures display autonomy and views independent of Jung's ego. In fact, most often, Jung does not agree with the inner figures, but through dialogue, he and they find a way to come to terms.

The other important capacity for the *opus* is *imaginatio* ("imagination"). As one alchemist counselled, "look according to nature, by which the bodies are regenerated in the bowels of the earth. And imagine this with the true and not with the fantastic imagination."[56] But what is "true imagination?" Here, *imaginatio* should be understood as a type of vision. One "sees" with the imagination, as one sees objects with the physical eye. According to Ruland's *Lexicon alchemiae*: "Imagination is the star in man, the celestial or supercelestial body."[57] This reference is to a spiritual sense with its source in the heavens, the supernatural realm of the spirit world. As the star is the guiding light for the mariner at sea, so too is imagination the guiding light for the explorer of the spiritual world, which Jung referred to as the unconscious. To explore the unconscious, imagination is key.

---

[56] Quoted by Jung in *CW* 12, para. 257, n. 36.
[57] Ibid., para. 394.

Imagination as a "faculty of the soul," Jung wrote quoting Sendivogius, involves both creativity and perception. As such, it has the capacity to create "something corporeal, a 'subtle body,' semi-spiritual in nature."[58] This differs from "fantastic imagination," which creates phantoms lacking in substance and importance—mere conceits or clever thoughts dressed as images, metaphors, or daydreams representing wish fulfilment. *Imaginatio* is the agency of the soul that creates symbols, which may take on semi-material form, as in visions. It does not spin aimless and groundless fantasies, but portrays invisible and immaterial facts in images true to their nature. This activity is an *opus*, "so the demand that the Artifex must have a sound physical constitution is quite intelligible, since he works with and through his own quintessence and is himself the indispensable condition of his own experiment."[59]

We must conceive of these imaginal objects not as mere fantasies, but as "subtle bodies" occupying "an intermediate realm between mind and matter."[60] About this "realm of subtle bodies," we cannot say that it is real or unreal. It is hybrid—half-spiritual, half-material. With the still-emergent notion of synchronicity and his conversations with Wolfgang Pauli about quantum physics and depth psychology in the back of his mind, Jung wrote:

---

[58] Ibid.
[59] Ibid.
[60] Ibid.

the moment when physics touches on the "untrodden, untreadable regions," and when psychology has at the same time to admit that there are other forms of psychic life besides the acquisition of personal consciousness – in other words, when psychology too touches on an impenetrable darkness – then the intermediate realm of subtle bodies comes to life again and the physical and the psychic are once more blended in an indissoluble unity. We have come very near to this turning point today.[61]

Through their use of *imaginatio*, the alchemists employed symbols with the power to transform material objects into representations of divine energy. This was the work of archetypal projection. Moreover, such symbols frequently constellated synchronicities—meaningful coincidences of psychic image and material object at a particular moment in time. This is the function of the *symbolon*—a classical term denoting the reunion of two related but separated halves of a single totality: matter and spirit. The *symbolon* creates a subtle body, inhabiting the intermediate space joining the two sides into a singular event.

---

[61] Ibid.

The alchemists often described *imaginatio* as the *astrum star*—a Paracelsan term meaning something like *quintessence*. They considered it a concentrated extract of the life force, both physical and psychic. They used *imaginatio* as a tool to grasp or call forth symbols from the darkness of the unconscious, which then served as a magical tokens for healing and transformation. On this basis, Jung considered *imaginatio* the most important key to understanding the *opus*.[62]

The notion that the psyche, through imagination, can create something in the mind that exerts an influence on external reality borders on what might traditionally be called "magic." In the context of psychological alchemy, this refers to the capacity of active imagination to establish living relationships with archetypal images and aspects of the Self. Such engagement has a profound effect on the individual's life and, in turn, their surroundings—not as the result of deliberate intention or conscious will, but through a more subtle "influence." Sometimes, this results in synchronicities, suggesting an underlying unity beyond the apparent dichotomy between psyche and matter. This, for Jung, is the "magic" of the alchemical *opus*. The imagination, when properly engaged, affects what takes place in the retort, and what takes place in the retort has an effect on the adept. There is a mutually creative interaction between mind and matter. The magic

---

[62] Ibid., para. 396.

is the mysterious power of the mind to transform mind and body through projection, meditation, and active imagination.

Lecture Four
Alchemy in a Dream Series

Alchemy describes a process of transformation from lower to higher states, from heavy and gross, like lead, to bright and refined, like gold or the much-admired *lapis philosophorum*. The alchemical transformation unfolds across stages of refinement aimed at drawing the essence, or soul, out of the darkness of matter. To speak of it in psychological terms, transformation involves the extraction of something hidden in the unconscious. In the beginning, there is a condition of darkness (*nigredo*) and confusion (*massa confusa*). Then, through the application of heat to the *vas* and patient work with the material contained within, the alchemist gradually extracts the valuable material, and the *prima materia* in the retort is transformed to a lighter condition (*albedo*). After that comes distillation of the essence, culminating in the golden stage (*rubedo*). The colors involved describe the progression of stages through a process of enlightenment as the alchemist moves from confusion and despair to the final goal, using the methods of *meditatio* and *imaginatio*.

The more noble alchemists understood the *opus* as both a chemical and a spiritual process. There were also lesser, more materialistic alchemists, who were just trying to make gold for the market and to become rich and famous. Jung was interested in the more sophisticated type of alchemist, working on the philosophical and spiritual plane, as much as the chemical. Such alchemists wrote of gold that is not gold, "*aurum non aurum,*" referring to spiritual attainment. Moreover, they described this with reverence, as if describing a numinous experience of the divine, or ultimate reality. Indeed, the words of the alchemists suggest mystical realizations.

Along with his general interest in exploring the developmental sequences of alchemy, Jung was searching for examples of a parallel process (in individuation), as experienced by his patients. The more instances of individuation he could identify across different historical periods and cultural contexts, the more firmly he could establish the process as archetypal (i.e., universal). His aim was to demonstrate that individuation is not only for the culturally elite, the highly educated, intellectual geniuses, or individuals of a specific cultural milieu, but a potential inherent in every person by virtue of possessing a human psyche. While each soul is unique in some respects, every soul is based on an archetypal ground that is universal and impersonal. It is this archetypal matrix that formed Jung's primary scientific interest.

In 1931, a young professor at the Federal Institute of Technology (ETH) in Zürich approached Jung for analysis, citing severe problems in his personal life. His name was Wolfgang Pauli—a brilliant mathematician who was already quite well known in the world of quantum physics.[63] Pauli was part of the team of physicists known as the Copenhagen School, alongside Niels Bohr, Albert Einstein, Werner Heisenberg, and others, who were probing into the subatomic levels of matter and coming up with amazing findings.

Wolfgang Pauli, age 29, before his class at the ETH.

---

[63] For biographical details, see Suzanne Gieser, *The Innermost Kernel*.

In his professional life, Pauli was doing extremely well. But his personal life was chaotic. His father, a professor at the University of Vienna who was troubled by his son's behavior, advised Pauli to see the famous Zürich psychoanalyst, C.G. Jung, about whom he had heard good things. Thus, it came to pass that Pauli asked Jung for treatment of his acute depression.

After meeting with Pauli once or twice, Jung concluded that it would be better if Pauli worked with a female analyst. He referred him to one of his young students, Erna Rosenbaum—an attractive young Austrian psychiatrist who was just beginning to practice as an analyst under Jung's guidance. The analysis, which started in February 1932, seemed to go well, lasting for five months in person, followed by three months of correspondence after Rosenbaum relocated to Berlin. During those eight months, Pauli recorded 355 dreams and visions. Subsequently, he began analysis with Jung, during which time he recorded another 45 dreams. Jung wrote that he offered no substantial interpretation of Pauli's dreams, due to "the dreamer's excellent scientific training and ability."[64] In other words, Pauli managed to interpret the dreams for himself, and Jung was present only as an observer.

From Pauli's first contact with Jung in 1931 until his death in 1958, the two maintained a meaningful

---

[64] Jung, *CW* 5, para. 45.

relationship, both in person and through correspondence. Their correspondence, which has now been published, includes substantial discussion of analytical psychology, the theory of archetypes, the relationship between depth psychology and quantum physics, and especially synchronicity—a phenomenon they both recognized as a meeting of psychology and modern physics.

By the time Pauli presented his dreams and visions to Jung, granting him permission to use them for scientific research, Jung was already deeply engaged in the study of alchemy. To his surprise, he found many parallels between Pauli's unconscious material and the alchemical images and processes found in the antique books he had been collecting and slowly working to understand. Both sets of material revealed the process of individuation, as Jung had previously theorized. This excited Jung's imagination, and at the Eranos Conference in 1935 he delivered his first lecture on Pauli's dream series, titled "*Traumsymbole des Individuationsprozesses*" ("Dream Symbols of the Individuation Process"). The following year (1936), during a visit to the United States, Jung expanded on this material in a series of lectures. After receiving an honorary doctorate at Harvard University's tercentenary celebration,[65] he traveled to Harbor Island, Maine, where he conducted a six-day seminar for the students of Esther Harding and Eleonore Bertine. He returned the next year

---

[65] Jung, "Psychological Factors Determining Human Behavior," *CW* 8.

to deliver another five-day seminar in New York, again focusing on Pauli's dreams.[66] Eventually, in 1944, Jung published his full commentary on the dream series as Part II of *Psychology and Alchemy*, which opens with the famous quotation from Virgil's *Aeneid*:

> ...easy is the descent to Avernus: night and day the door of gloomy Dis stands open; but to recall the steps and pass out to the upper air, this is the task, this the toil.[67]

Aeneas, like Odysseus before him, descended to the underworld to consult with the ancestors and receive guidance for his journey. This was a hero's journey to discover a personal destiny. Of this journey, Jung wrote:

> The dread and resistance which every natural human being experiences when it comes to delving too deeply into himself is, at bottom, the fear of the journey to Hades....The psychological danger that arises here is the disintegration of personality into its functional

---

[66] Gieser, ed., *C.G. Jung, Dream Symbols of the Individuation Process, Notes of C.G. Jung's Seminar on Wolfgang Pauli's Dreams*, 1.
[67] Trans. by H.R. Fairclough, quoted by Jung, *CW* 12, para. 39.

components, i.e., the separate functions of consciousness, the complexes, hereditary units, etc…that is to say, the body and the psychic representatives of the organs gain mastery over the conscious mind. In the hero myth this state is known as being swallowed up in the belly of the whale or dragon. The heat here is so intense that the hero loses his hair.[68]

Obviously, Jung thought of Pauli's dream series as a journey into the underworld of the unconscious. On the other hand, Pauli did not seem to feel the resistance described by Aeneas when he began his analysis with Erna Rosenberg. He entered willingly and enthusiastically,

---

[68] Ibid., paras. 439–440.

and he produced a rich trove of *prima materia* for the alchemical *opus* that lay ahead of him.

There are numerous versions of the alchemical process, but they all share certain common features. For instance, the process must begin with the *prima materia*. Without this, the *opus* cannot achieve its highest aim—alchemical gold—no matter how hard the alchemist fans the flames of his furnace. Indeed, the texts agree that one must start with this basic material, out of which everything is made, and it must be collected carefully, hence the secret recipes passed down through generations. The *prima materia* is the "first matter," or "original stuff." It contains the germ seed for the celebrated tree that will grow in the *vas*. It is the *increatum*, the uncreated. In analysis, we find it in the collection of material from the unconscious, such as the dreams and images that appear in the course of the psychological *opus*.

Jung often cautioned that such *prima materia*, which he interpreted as the collective unconscious, is potentially hazardous. It is a place where dragons dwell and one can get lost, or certainly disoriented. It can destroy the ego, fragment the persona, and open the doors to unbearable anguish and depression. But to some extent, all this *must* happen if the process is to get going. For this reason, the alchemists celebrated the *nigredo* when it appeared. It was the signal of the beginning of the process. As many have said, analysis is a controlled psychosis. This was certainly Jung's own experience during midlife, as recorded and published in *The Red Book*.

In his essay "Psychological Commentary on *The Tibetan Book of the Dead*," published in 1935 (around the same time Jung was working intensively on Pauli's dreams) Jung wrote that the journey into the unconscious involves a dangerous reversal of the aims and intentions of the conscious mind. It demands a sacrifice of ego dominance and a surrender to the uncertainty of what must seem like a chaotic riot of phantasmal forms.[69] However, after one has spent some time in the unconscious and gotten used to the dark, one may discover order in the material.

When studying Pauli's dreams, Jung sought to identify signs of an archetypal process of individuation emerging from the unconscious. He approached the material as a scientific investigation, adopting the stance of an objective and disinterested observer. For the final publication in *Psychology and Alchemy*, he distilled the extensive corpus of 400 dreams to a curated selection of eighty-one. The resulting text is characteristically Jungian in scope and depth, reflecting a fascinating, rich, and complex synthesis of Pauli's unconscious material (dreams and visions), alchemical images and ideas, amplifications from myths across cultures, and psychological theory.

In his commentary, Jung employed alchemy as a hermeneutic framework for interpreting the symbolic

---

[69] Jung, "Psychological Commentary on *The Tibetan Book of the Dead*," *CW* 11, para. 849.

content of Pauli's dreams and visions, which he addressed in two principle sections. The first section, titled "The Initial Dreams," shows the beginning of the process to come. The second, titled "The Symbolism of the Mandala," concentrates on the emergence of mandala images as they occur in the series. Here, I have chosen four of Jung's commentaries to discuss. The first, relating to Dream #1 (from "The Initial Dreams" section),[70] shows the beginning of Pauli's journey into the unconscious. The second, which concerns Dream #13 (from "The Mandalas in Dreams" section),[71] represents Pauli's descent into the waters of the unconscious. Dream #23 from the same section[72] symbolizes the alchemical *opus* itself. And finally, "The Great Vision"—or as it is better known, "The World Clock Vision"[73]—concludes Jung's commentary on the series.

Dream #1 is short: "The dreamer is at a social gathering. On leaving, he puts on a stranger's hat instead of his own."[74] This doesn't seem like a very promising beginning for an individuation process, but Jung understood this "putting on a stranger's hat" in a very special way: Pauli's mistake is the necessary step that initiates his individuation process. He leaves his old hat at the party and, by putting on another, signals a shift in his identity.

---

[70] Jung, *CW* 12, para. 52.
[71] Ibid., para. 154.
[72] Ibid., para. 212.
[73] Ibid., para. 307.
[74] Ibid., para. 52.

In his discussion of this dream, Jung referred to Gustav Meyrink's novel, *The Golem*, in which the hero puts on the hat of Athanasius Pernath and becomes involved in strange supernatural experiences. The name "Athanasius," in Greek, means "immortal." Thus, the hat of Athanasius, who is a being beyond time, changes the consciousness of the wearer into the universal and everlasting man (the Self), as distinct from the ephemeral and accidental mortal man (the ego). This is an astonishing leap of interpretation.

Jung placed great significance on this dream, as it was an initial dream. For Jung, the initial dream in analysis holds high symbolic value. It may not look like much, but neither does the *prima materia*. It's something you find in the streets, as common as dung in the alleys of a medieval city.

As Jung took up the symbol of the hat in Pauli's dream, he noted that it was round, like the solar disc or a crown. This hat represents the first mandala in the series, and, as such, it puts the dreamer in contact with the immortal self—his soul—the part of him that is beyond time and space, not ephemeral, not accidental. The attribute of timelessness is confirmed in the ninth dream in the mandala series, while the circular character of the hat re-emerges in the thirty-fifth mandala dream. Thus, Pauli's initial dream foreshadows what is to come.

Jung studied this dream series with great care, much as he did the alchemical texts accumulating in his library at the time. Most likely, he created an index of recurring motifs—words, phrases, and images—much like the index he compiled for his alchemical research. In his commentary, he noted that the round image appears across multiple dreams in the series. This repetition signaled to him a purposive movement of the unconscious pushing its way into consciousness, through repeated images and figures standing like a shadow behind the dreamer. Thus, what Jung found in the first dream marked an auspicious beginning.

Dream #13 is more obviously symbolic. Pauli dreams there is treasure in the sea. To reach it, he must dive through a narrow opening, representing a dangerous transition from the personal to the collective unconscious. The dreamer takes the plunge into the dark waters, and he discovers a beautiful garden in the depths, symmetrically laid out with a fountain in the center. This is the appearance of order within the *massa confusa*, the sea. The fountain at the center—also a mandala image—may have reminded Jung of his "Liverpool dream," which was the culmination of his quest for a personal myth.[75] Likewise, Jung noted that this dream seems to be introducing the dreamer to an initial image of the Self in the depths of the unconscious.

Moving to **Dream #23**, we find the dreamer in a square space. Jung was very careful about noting the geometry of objects and spaces in Pauli's dreams: Was it square? Was it circular? Or was it rectangular? He spoke of a rectangular image as a distorted square, possibly

---

[75] Jung, *Memories, Dreams, Reflections*, 196–97.

compensating the conscious attitude of the dreamer. A square is, of course, a symbol of the Self. In this dream, the dreamer sits opposite an unknown woman, whose portrait he is supposed to be drawing. This woman has already appeared in several earlier dreams, and now the dreamer is looking directly at her. Strangely, however, what he draws is not her face, but three-leaf clovers (or distorted crosses) in four colors—red, yellow, green, and blue. The dreamer seems engaged in squaring the circle, using both triadic (the clovers) and quaternary (the four colors) symbolism. In alchemy, this movement between three and four is associated with the emergence of the *lapis philosophorum*. Following this dream, Pauli began drawing circles divided into quarters with a four-petalled blue flower in the center—a new mandala image—thereby solidifying his dream experience of squaring the circle.

In his commentary on this significant dream of anima and integration, Jung expounded on the topic of *imaginatio* in alchemy as "the real and literal power to create images." "Imaginatio," he wrote, "is the active evocation of (inner) images *secundum naturam*, an authentic feat of thought or ideation, which does not spin aimless and groundless fantasies into the blue' – does not, that is to say, just play with its objects, but tries to grasp the inner facts and portray them in images true to their nature. This activity is an *opus*, a work."[76] This

---

[76] Ibid., para. 219.

aptly describes what the alchemists were doing in their laboratories and what Pauli was doing with his drawings. We may also be reminded of Jung's own engagement with active imagination for *The Red Book*, when he explored the depths of the collective unconscious and rendered these "inner facts...in images true to their nature." This was all part of his *opus* of individuation.

Pauli was also engaged in this *opus*, as is evident in his dreams and visions. Jung concluded his commentary on this extraordinary body of material with a discussion of Pauli's "Great Vision"—a culminating symbolic image integrating the preceding dream motifs.

In this final vision, Pauli describes two intersecting circles—one vertical, one horizontal—converging at a common center. This configuration forms the "World Clock," representing a cosmic mandala of time and space. The entire structure is supported by a black bird.[77]

---

[77] Ibid., para. 307.

Jung regarded this vision as a profound and magnificent prefiguration of the Self in Pauli's imaginal experience. The black bird is a frequent symbol of the alchemical and hermaphroditic Mercurius, who the alchemists regarded as both the beginning and the end of the process: the *prima materia,* the *lapis philosophorum.* Mercurius personifies the spirit of the unconscious itself, and his presence as the supporting figure in this vision imbues it with foundational psychological significance.

As an image emerging from the unconscious, the "World Clock" was a symbolic gift intended for integration into Pauli's conscious attitude. But why a clock? A clock indicates timing, but this clock seems to extend beyond our normal sense of time as past, present, and future, and seems to anticipate the concept of synchronicity, upon which Pauli and Jung would elaborate in the decades to follow. Here, time is conveyed as a convergence of time and eternity, signifying the emergence of meaning in time—for both the individual and the collective.

The vertical circle—a blue disc with a white border—is subdivided into $4 \times 8 = 32$ segments, over which a pointer rotates. Although this mechanism resembles a conventional clock, its thirty-two positions distinguish it as a symbolic timepiece of an entirely different order. The horizontal circle consists of four colors and supports four little men holding pendulums, emphasizing the quaternity. Surrounding this circle is a ring that, having once been dark, now appears golden. The clock has three rhythms, or pulses. The smallest pulse advances the pointer on the blue vertical disc by one increment (1/32); the middle pulse completes a full revolution of the pointer, causing the horizontal plane to rotate by one segment (1/32); and the great pulse—consisting of thirty-two middle pulses—results in a full revolution of the horizontal plane and the golden ring. This visionary construction evoked in Pauli the impression of "the most sublime harmony."[78]

In his commentary on this remarkable vision, Jung interpreted it as an authentic manifestation of the Self—the organizing center and encompassing totality of the psyche. The image functions as a mandala that "aspires to the most complete union of opposites that is possible, including that of the masculine trinity and the feminine quaternity."[79] Jung saw it as "a small-scale model or perhaps even a source of space-time...four-dimensional in nature although only visible in a three-dimensional projection."[80] Jung had followed the emergence of mandala images throughout Pauli's dream series, and this culminating vision—depicting a mandala in embodied, spatial form—signified to him psychic realization and integration. With this symbol, Jung felt that Pauli had achieved psychic balance and a new center. "What a man does in reality, he himself becomes,"[81] wrote Jung, affirming his belief that true imagination is a transformative

---

[78] Ibid., para. 308.
[79] Ibid., para. 311.
[80] Ibid., para. 312.
[81] Ibid., para. 308.

function—one capable of creating or discovering symbols from the unconscious and bringing them into the light of consciousness. This imaginative operation, so essential to the *opus*, was enacted by both the alchemists and modern individuals such as Pauli and Jung himself.

Lecture Five
The Alchemy of Transcendence in Relationship

Coniunctio, or the union of opposites, is a central theme in alchemy. Most frequently, the theme is depicted as a union of male and female figures. In "The Psychology of the Transference," Jung focused precisely on this topic, using a selection of images and statements from the alchemical text *Rosarium Philosophorum*. In this essay, two of Jung's primary interests flow together: the study of alchemy and the phenomenon of transference, as it occurs in psychoanalysis and beyond. As he did with the dreams and visions of Wolfgang Pauli (discussed in the previous lecture), Jung employed alchemy as a hermeneutic instrument to discuss the complexities of the analytical relationship and the transformation it facilitates for both analyst and analysand. He framed this dynamic in terms of the alchemical *coniunctio*—a symbolic union capturing the psychological interpenetration of subjectivities. Crucially, Jung observed that this process is not confined to clinical analysis, but also occurs in non-clinical contexts.

Transference in Analysis

Jung's initial interest in the phenomenon of transference can be traced back to his tenure as a resident psychiatrist at the Burghölzli Clinic in Zürich. At the instigation of Prof. Eugen Bleuler, he became acquainted with the writings of Sigmund Freud, which prompted a pivotal journey to Vienna in 1907, alongside his wife, Emma, his colleague Ludwig Binswanger, and one of his daughters, Hilde.[82] During one of their many intense discussions, Freud posed the question: "Dr. Jung, how do you understand the transference?" Jung replied immediately, "Oh, the transference is all." Freud nodded sagely and said: "You have understood." In Freud's view, the transference relationship was central to psychoanalysis, providing a gateway to the unconscious, and especially (for Freud) repressed childhood fantasies regarding erotic love for parental figures. By analyzing the recurrence of these Oedipal patterns within the analytical relationship, the analyst could access a patient's early memory fragments and pull them up into consciousness. Doing so would reveal the source of the patient's neurosis, allowing it to be worked through and resolved. This is why Jung said the transference was "all"—a "love cure," as psychoanalysis came to be known.

Two decades later, in 1929, Jung wrote an article titled "Problems of Modern Psychotherapy," in

---

[82] Freud and Jung, *The Freud-Jung Letters*, 24.

which he considered the "love cure" once again. In the paper, he articulated a more nuanced understanding of the therapeutic process, distinguishing between the approaches of Freud, Adler, and his own. He also proposed a model consisting of four stages of analysis. In this model, the first stage, "confession," involves the analysand's disclosure of deeply personal material, often for the first time. The act of verbalizing these secrets in the presence of a non-judgmental analyst tends to elicit emotional relief, as the analysand is supported in the process of coming to terms with the secret experiences and integrating them into their psychological reality, at which point they may proceed on their individuation journey. Some patients describe this stage as "cleaning out the basement." The second stage, "elucidation," corresponds most closely with the Freudian approach. Here, the analyst offers psychodynamic interpretations of the analysand's complex emotional reactions and attitudes. These interpretations elucidate some of the unconscious scaffolding of the analysand's emotional functioning, generally consisting of early childhood experiences and unresolved traumas. Such insights may alleviate distress by fostering a deeper cognitive understanding of the inner dynamics at play. The third stage, "education," is closely associated with Adler. Adler's school had a very strong social orientation and was engaged in assisting educational institutions to improve psychological hygiene. Thus, this stage refers to a cognitive intervention aimed at enhancing the analysand's understanding of their psychological functioning and relation to broader society. The analyst assumes a pedagogical role, recommending books or educational opportunities that the analysand might benefit from, gaining clarity and orientation in their life circumstances.

The fourth and final phase of psychotherapy, "transformation," marks the Jungian contribution. This stage involves profound engagement with the dynamics of transference and countertransference in the relationship between analyst and analysand. Jung conceived of this stage as a deeply reciprocal process, with both individuals affected by the psychological interaction. He emphasized the mutual nature of the therapeutic encounter, likening it to an alchemical process in which both participants undergo psychological change. If sustained over time, this mutual engagement can catalyze continued individual and psychological growth for both parties.

A decade later, alchemy entered the discussion of transformation in analysis when Jung wrote the important essay, "Psychology of the Transference." Drawing on imagery from the alchemical text *Rosarium Philosophorum* ("The Rosary of the Philosophers"), Jung deepened his reflections on the nature of the transformation process as it unfolds within the transference relationship.

The *Rosarium Philosophorum*

The earliest printed edition of the *Rosarium Philosophorum* was titled *De Alchimia* and published in

Frankfurt in 1550. It was based on a hand-copied manuscript attributed to Arnold de Villanova, a well-known alchemist of the thirteenth century. The term *rosarium* in Latin refers to both a "rosary" and a "rose garden." The familiar Catholic Rosary, developed in the Middle Ages as a means for contemplation and prayer, consists of a series of prayers recited routinely and repeatedly by the devout. It is meant as an aid to focus the mind on Christ, the gospels, and religious images. Similarly, the *Rosarium Philosophorum* consists of a sequence of twenty emblematic images designed to guide the alchemist or philosopher through meditative contemplation. Each plate is accompanied by commentary by renowned alchemical thinkers.

Jung's essay blends three parallel lines of discussion. The first refers to the alchemical *opus* itself, showing the union of King and Queen (i.e., solar and lunar energies) to form a "Rebis"—a symbol of integration. In alchemy, the Rebis is also known as the *filius philosophorum* ("the son of the philosophers") or the *lapis philosophorum* ("the stone of the philosophers"). Concretely, this is an object with magical properties that can transform base metals into gold and heal all diseases. However, the philosophical alchemists also wrote about spiritual development, and this represents Jung's second line of thought. The more spiritual and philosophical alchemists wrote of gold that is not really gold, or a lapis that is not really stone. Thus, two levels of the alchemical *opus*—one material/chemical and another psychological/ spiritual—came into play in their writings.

The third interpretative strand in Jung's essay is clinical, concerning the dynamics of the transference relationship that unfolds within the *temenos* of the analytic setting. On this point, Jung was writing as a seasoned clinician with extensive experience of transference relationships. Many of those who came to work with Jung likely did so with a strong transference already in place—either on a personal level (manifesting as a positive or negative father complex) or on an archetypal level (viewing him as a magician, superman, or sage). Jung sought to understand transference not merely as a repetition of past attachments, but as a transformative psychological process that takes place within the protected space of analysis. It is especially for this purpose that he turned to the images of the *Rosarium Philosophorum* for amplification.

As described above, the *Rosarium Philosophorum* consists of twenty images. Jung's commentary is limited to the first ten. The initial five images depict the evolving relationship between a King and a Queen, beginning with their formal meeting, progressing through their mutual learning about one other, and culminating in their intimate sexual relationship. This sequence is followed by two images symbolizing a state of liminality or incubation, which Jung emphasizes in his text. Finally, images eight through ten portray the emergence of a new being through this *coniunctio*. This triadic structure—

encounter, incubation, and transformation—provides the basic framework for Jung's exploration of the transference relationship in analysis.

The *Rosarium Philosophorum* Images

Plate #1: The Setting

The *Rosarium Philosophorum* opens with an image depicting the setting for the drama to come, the Mercurial Fountain.

ROSARIVM

In this image, the fountain is surrounded by four stars in the four corners and a fifth star in the center between sun and moon. Inscribed beneath the twin serpent heads at the top are the Latin words *mineralis, vegetabilis,* and *animalis*. Jung wrote that "*vegetabilis* should be translated as 'living' and *animalis* as 'animate' in the sense of having a soul, or even as psychic"[83]—referring to the threefold manifestation of Mercurius, the agent of transformation in alchemy. The fountain itself, contained within a secure structure, serves as the vessel, or *vas,* for the alchemical *opus,* thus constituting a sacred space or *temenos*. From its three spigots flow symbolic liquids: *lac virginis* (virgin's milk), *acetum fontis* (spring vinegar), and *aqua vitae* (water of life).

The text for this image reads:

We are the beginning and first nature of metals,
Art by us maketh the highest tincture.
There is no fountain nor water found like unto me.
I heal both the poor and the rich,
But yet I am full of hurtful poison.

The "highest tincture" produced by "the art" is endowed with powerful healing and transformative power. The Mercurial Fountain depicted here is unique and unparalleled: it is said to heal both rich and poor, alike, signifying its universality and accessibility. However, this inclusivity is accompanied by a caution. Though open to all, it contains a potent poison—*Mercurius*, or mercury—

---

[83] Jung, "The Psychology of the Transference," para. 402.

which, while symbolically redemptive, is literally toxic. Thus, the image issues both an invitation and a warning: this fountain is available to everyone, but you better know what you are doing when you enter it, because it can be very destructive.

The inscriptions around the fountain name the *prima materia* in its three forms— *Mercurius mineralis*, *Mercurius vegitabilis*, and *Mercurius animalis*— affirming that these are ultimately one and the same. In this triadic unity, Mercurius encompasses all parts of the natural world—mineral, vegetable, and animal. As a unifying archetype, Mercurius is present at the beginning, throughout, and at the culmination of the *opus*. He flows from the spouts of the fountain, as: *lac virginis* (virgin's milk), representing the feminine principle; *acetum fontis* (spring vinegar), representing the masculine principle; and *aqua vitae* (water of life), representing the vital synthesis of the two. Vinegar is corrosive, sharp, and fiery. However, combined with virgin's milk, it becomes the water of life (*aqua vitae*)—the source of the soul's energy. Together, these three essences—feminine, masculine, and life-giving—constitute the core elements with which the alchemists engaged in the transformation process.

Plate #2: King and Queen

In the second image of the *Rosarium Philosophorum*, we see two human figures, a King and a Queen, standing on the sun and moon, respectively. As royalty, they represent archetypes of the collective unconscious. They are what we call "dominants"—figures inherent in every human psyche.

PHILOSOPHORVM.

In this image, the King, standing upon the sun, represents the dominant of the collective consciousness, while the Queen, poised on the moon, represents the dominant of the collective unconscious. Their gestures of greeting mark a significant moment—the initial encounter between conscious and unconscious realms. Each figure holds a flower in the right hand, their stems crossing in a gesture of mutual offering, while a dove descends from above, bearing a third branch. This visual triad alludes to the three streams depicted in the earlier image of the Mercurial Fountain (virgin's milk, spring vinegar, and the water of life). The dove, symbolizing the transcendent Holy Spirit, augurs well for this meeting. Indeed, the friendly masculine agency of the King, the equally friendly receptivity of the Queen, and the supportive presence of the transcendent Self sets the stage for movement toward individuation.

The left-handed handshake between the King and Queen suggests a secret relationship between them already at this stage. As animus and anima, they were once united within the Self, preceding the differentiation of consciousness and unconsciousness. Their reunion at this stage evokes that original kinship, now manifesting as a *syzygy*—a brother/sister pair—which symbolically implies an incestuous union. Jung referred to this as "the smell of incest," signaling an intimate and secretive collusion in the service of psychological transformation.

This condition metaphorically reflects the psychic state of individuals entering analysis at midlife—a period when conscious and unconscious elements seek renewed and more integrated contact. The analytic *temenos* offers the necessary container for this transformative engagement, enabling a reconfiguration of personality. Notably, this was the case with the young Wolfgang Pauli, whose analytical work with Jung and Erna Rosenbaum generated an extraordinary series of dreams and visions that vividly traced the stages of individuation (as explored in the previous lecture).

At this point in his discussion of the transference, Jung introduced the following diagram to clarify the relational dynamics involved:

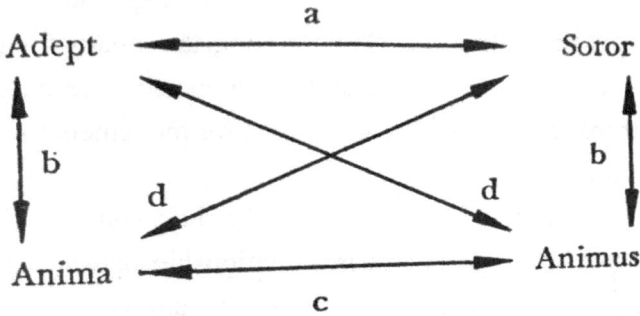

For the purposes of this discussion, these figures may be understood as analyst (A) and patient (P), as illustrated in the following diagram:

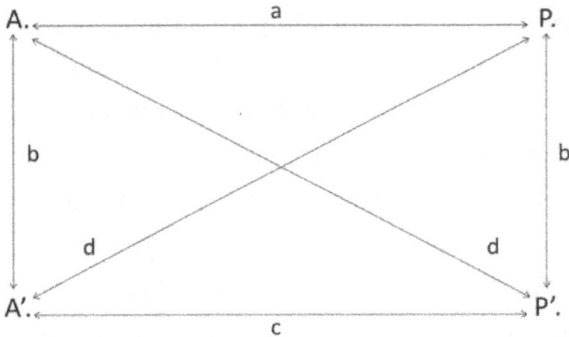

Vector "a" indicates a relatively uncomplicated conscious relationship between analyst (A) and patient (P), as partners working together on a joint project (i.e., analysis). This includes a professional agreement whereby the analyst commits to perform services in a professional and ethical way for the patient's benefit, and the patient agrees to the logistical terms of the treatment, such as session timing, frequency, and fees. Thus, a professional relationship is established at the outset and ideally sustained throughout the analytic engagement.

Vector "b," by contrast, refers to the intrapsychic dimension operative in both analyst and patient. In Jung's diagram, it is obvious that he assumed a male analyst and female patient. Thus, on the intrapsychic level, vector "b" represents the relationship between the analyst's ego and his unconscious (anima), and between the patient's ego and her unconscious (animus). This dynamic encompasses the presence of autonomous complexes within each participant. These often-unspoken internal influences—which might be considered shadow material— may include feelings of anger, envy, and fear rooted in each individual's personal history, which can significantly complicate the analytical relationship.

Vector "c" is the most psychologically compelling for our purposes, forming the focal point of Jung's essay. It is at this level that the *coniunctio* relationship between King and Queen, as depicted in the *Rosarium Philosophorum*—and by extension, the analytic dyad— takes place. Here, unconscious meets unconscious, anima encounters animus. This dynamic affects both parties in the analytic relationship and operates independently of the conscious intentions and agreements reflected at level "a." When individuals form a close bond, whether in analysis or in other forms of deep relational engagement, they begin to share psychic content and experiences that are uncanny and unexpected. These may manifest as synchronicities, parallel dreams, mutual interests, or overlapping life histories. A sense of intuitive recognition of the other as a "soulmate" can emerge, associated with the feeling that each person can sense the other's thoughts and emotions even before the other does. Within the analytic context, such experiences may come as a great surprise, inducing a kind of trancelike state in the relationship that may be particularly palpable and impactful.

Vector "d" represents the classic transference path: the woman's unconscious (animus) is projected onto the man, and the man's unconscious (anima) is projected onto the woman. This dynamic creates a false bond that is eventually shattered by the reality of the personalities involved. Only once this projection is withdrawn can a more realistic and grounded relationship emerge. Importantly, however, the dissolution of this transference does not negate or diminish the deeper processes unfolding along vector "c."

Jung's term for the psychic energy that fuels this deep, unconscious relationship was "kinship libido." He wrote: "This is the core of the transference phenomenon… behind it stands the restless urge towards individuation."[84]

---

[84] Jung, "The Psychology of the Transference," paras. 445–46.

Plate #3: The Naked Truth

Jung aptly titled the third picture of the *Rosarium Philosophorum* "The Naked Truth."

The image depicts the couple at the moment of mutual proposal and acceptance of marriage. The King declares, "O Luna, let me be thy husband," to which the Queen replies, "O Sol, I submit to thee." Both parties express their wishes and intentions with what Jung described as "unabashed naturalness." Hovering above them, the dove bears the inscription *Spiritus est qui unificat* ("this is the

Spirit that unifies"). A footnote in the text reminds us that the dove "is also an attribute of the goddess of love and was a symbol of *amor coniungalis* in ancient times."[85]

Because this alchemical couple represents the unconscious relationship between analyst and patient, we must bear in mind that it expresses the interaction between the anima and animus. On the conscious level (especially within traditional patriarchal societies), the man represents the dominant figure in the couple, while at the unconscious level, his anima submits to the animus of the woman. Jung argued that this dynamic also plays out in the transference relationship in analysis. As we see in the later pictures, however, these roles of dominance and submission are not fixed. In the first part of the series, the King is positioned above the Queen during coitus (Picture 5), while in the second part of the series, the Queen is positioned above the King in their conjugal embrace (Picture 11). Jung interpreted this positionality as corresponding to the locus of psychic transformation, with the partner undergoing the deeper process of change occupying the dominant position within the dynamic.

Plate #4: Immersion in the Bath

The King and Queen, still wearing their crowns of identity, are now seated in the Mercurial Fountain. They remain at a respectful distance, holding the flowers that

---

[85] Ibid., para. 238, n. 7.

signify the continued ritual of union. The dove once again appears above them, accompanying them in this next step toward *conjunctio*.

The couple are about to undergo what Jung called a "night sea journey"—a descent into the waters of the unconscious, where they will undergo a dissolution of personal boundaries (*solutio*) and become one. With respect to the analytic process, this phase might correspond to a deepening of the transference relationship, reflecting a commitment by both analyst and analysand to the transformative process. At such a junction, there is no turning back. The King and Queen are reaching that decisive moment. They are about to gain full knowledge of one another. As Dorn wrote: "As bodies are dissolved through the solution, so the doubts of the philosophers are resolved through knowledge."[86] The presence of the dove in this scene "signalizes the meaning of their relationship: [the] longing for transcendent wholeness," as Jung indicated.[87]

Plate #5: The Conjunction

We now see the King and Queen underwater, with their bodies energetically entwined in a full conjugal embrace. Jung's commentary on this image judiciously reminds us that we should look upon the act as symbolic, rather than carnal. The figures appear quite determined to complete the *coniunctio* as promised in the previous images. Sun and moon look on in the background.

---

[86] Ibid., para. 241, n. 1.
[87] Ibid., para. 456.

The accompanying text reads: "O Luna, folded in my sweet embrace, you are made as strong and mighty as I." She replies: "O Sol, brightest of all lights, and yet you need me as the cock the hen." In response to this image, Jung drew attention to a line from the *Rosarium*: "*In hora coniunctionis maxima apparent miracula*" ("In the hour of conjunction the greatest miracles appear"). The miracle alluded to is the conception of the soul, which is born of this symbolic union and will enter the unfolding drama in the following scene.

Jung inserted image 11 of the *Rosarium* here, which again shows the King and Queen in coitus, but winged and with the Queen in the upper position.

His aim, in doing so, was to emphasize the spiritual nature of the *coniunctio* in the context of the transference relationship. In the *Rosarium Philosophorum*, this image is titled *Fermentatio* ("fermentation"). The King and Queen have now been "sublimated" and appear as vaporous forms. In the alchemical retort, this would correspond to the steam rising from the *prima materia*, condensing at the top and forming droplets of moisture to be distilled into a new, more potent substance. This emergent substance will ultimately become the *alexipharmikon*—the healing elixir—as we shall see in later images. Spiritually and psychologically, the image signifies an experience of the Self. For Jung, this stage illustrated the union of consciousness and unconsciousness in the analytical relationship, as the two psyches mingle and come into intimate contact. Thus, the intrapsychic and the interpersonal dimensions of analysis are inextricably linked, each depending upon and deepening the other.

Plate #6: Death

The King and Queen, now united in one body, lie quietly as though in a coffin. Jung titled this image "Death."

The *Rosarium*, however, named this image *conceptio* and *putrificatio* ("conception" and "putrefaction" or "corruption"). The accompanying text states: "Here King and Queen are lying dead / In great distress the soul is sped." The image marks a significant tonal shift, with

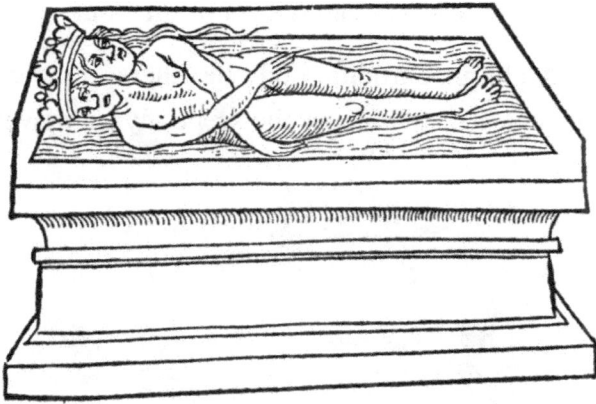

the excited eroticism of the previous scene giving way to stillness and repose. The two personalities have merged to form one body with two heads. The left side of the hermaphrodite is feminine, while the right is masculine, preserving a symbolic differentiation within the unity of their new form. The fire of desire has subsided, and the *coniuncio* has culminated in death—the necessary dissolution that precedes transformation. Jung interpreted this moment as a critical transitional phase: "this death is an interim stage to be followed by a new life. No new life can arise, say the alchemists, without the death of the old."[88] At this junction, things are quiet, but one can imagine the two heads communicating quietly with one another in a type of liminal exchange. Integration has taken place between the royal pair, the anima and animus. However, the process is not yet complete.

---

[88] Ibid., para. 467.

Plate #7: The Ascent of the Soul

While the hermaphroditic body lies there in the coffin, a newly begotten soul leaves the scene, flying upward into the heavens.

This stage represents the nadir of the alchemical process—a moment of utter desolation in which the soul has departed, leaving behind only a lifeless corpse. In this phase, the alchemists described the separation of elements and the grinding down of components into complete blackness: "Here is the division of the four elements / As from the lifeless corpse the soul ascends." The alchemist Arnoldus wrote: "When the first is black we say it is the key of the work, because it is not done without blackness."[89]

---

[89] McLean, *The Rosary of the Philosophers*, p. 45.

In his commentary, Jung emphasized the psychic danger in this state of soul loss, writing:

> This picture corresponds psychologically to a dark state of disorientation. The decomposition of the elements indicates dissociation and the collapse of the existing ego-consciousness. It is closely analogous to the schizophrenic state, and it should be taken very seriously because this is the moment when latent psychoses may become acute, i.e., when the patient becomes aware of the collective unconscious and the psychic non-ego. This collapse and disorientation of consciousness may last a considerable time, and it is one of the most difficult transitions the analyst has to deal with, demanding the greatest patience, courage, and faith on the part of both doctor and patient. It is a sign that the patient is being driven along willy-nilly without any sense of direction, that, in the truest sense of the word, he is in an utterly soulless condition, exposed to the full force of autoerotic affects and fantasies. Referring to this state of deadly darkness, one alchemist says: "Hoc est ergo magnum signum, in cuius investigatione nonnulli perierunt"

(This is a great sign, in the investigation
of which not a few have perished).[90]

Paradoxically, although this stage is described as the
key to the *opus*—marking the profound encounter with
the collective unconscious and the suffering through its
powerful energies—it is also the most fraught with danger.
When Jung foresaw the possibility of unleashing latent
psychoses in seemingly normal and conventional patients
in analysis, he politely counseled them not to undertake
the risks of such a night sea journey. As he wrote, this
critical moment in the individuation process tests the
analyst's faith in the psyche's capacity for transformation
and rebirth. Elsewhere, I have written about this "faith of
the analyst": "The analyst must be knowledgeable about
the death-and-rebirth archetype. But this must be Gnosis,
i.e., knowledge based on the analyst's own experience,
otherwise it is not effective or strong enough to hold the
analyst's confidence and trust in the process."[91]

If this image were the end of the story, it would be
a disaster. It would depict the worst possible outcome in a
therapeutic relationship—stuckness, lifelessness, loss of
soul, and inability to function—with both parties lying at
the bottom of a coffin-like container. Fortunately, this is
not the final scene in the *Rosarium Philosophorum*.

---

[90] Jung, "The Psychology of the Transference," para. 476.
[91] Stein, "The Faith of the Analyst," 253–54.

Plate #8: Purification

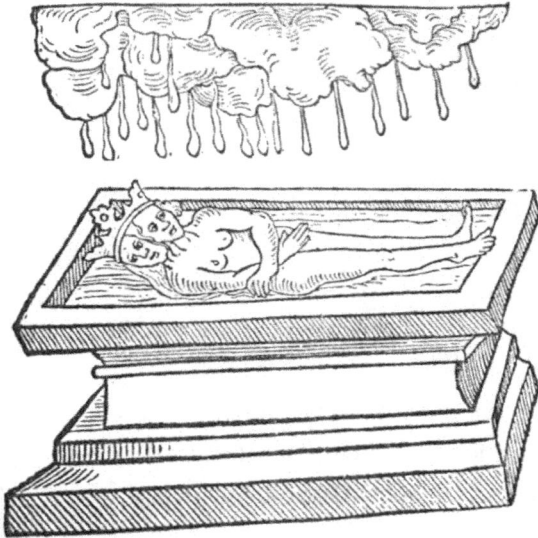

In this picture, we see water falling from the clouds above onto the lifeless body resting in the coffin. The text reads: "Here falls the heavenly dew, to lave / The soiled black body in the grave." This moment marks the onset of the *albedo*, representing the whitening or purification stage of the alchemical *opus*. It is analogous to the first light of dawn that illuminates the sky and makes objects in the surrounding world visible. As Jung wrote: "The spirit Mercurius descends in his heavenly form as *sapientia* and as the fire of the Holy Ghost to purify the blackness."[92] This whitening augurs new life for the hermaphroditic body lying supine in the coffin. Thus, the image represents

---

[92] Jung, "The Psychology of the Transference," para. 484.

a dramatic change, "an enantiodromia: the *nigredo* gives way to the *albedo*."[93]

Jung described this as a critically important phase in the individuation process. It is the stage in which the ego is cleansed of its entanglement with the archetypal contents of the collective unconscious that have surfaced and attached themselves to it. This purification enables the ego to differentiate itself more fully and to stand in mature relation to the unconscious. As the alchemist Senior wrote, "The spirit enters not into bodies unless the bodies be clean."[94]

In his commentary, Jung wrote of the danger of becoming identified with the unity previously achieved, which forms the hermaphroditic being in the coffin. If the consciousness of either party falls into this condition, they will become grotesquely inflated and lose their sense of reality. Consciousness must be washed, cleansed, and stripped of this temptation, using water to dissolve the glue that pastes ego to archetype. "In alchemy the purification is the result of numerous distillations; in psychology too, it comes from an equally thorough separation of the ordinary ego-personality from all inflationary admixtures of unconscious material. This task entails the most painstaking self-examination and self-education."[95] However, "by this light it will be possible to see what the real meaning of that union was."[96]

---

[93] Ibid., para. 493.
[94] McLean, *The Rosary of the Philosophers*, 52.
[95] Jung, *"The Psychology of the Transference,"* para. 503.
[96] Ibid., para. 493.

Plate #9: The Return of the Soul

In this image, the once-departed soul is shown descending alongside the falling rain, returning to the lifeless body in order to revivify it.

The accompanying text reads: "Here the soul descends from on high / To quicken the corpse that was purified."[97] Jung interpreted this as follows: "The 'soul' which is reunited with the body is the One born of the two, the *vinculum* common to both. It is therefore the very essence of relationship."[98] It is this factor that reanimates the corpse and brings life back to the couple. It is also the guarantee of the bond's permanence. The revitalized body of the couple is the product of an unconscious process emanating from the Self. All of this takes place in the non-ego area of the psyche, and is not to be confused with a "mere love-affair

---

[97] Ibid., para. 285. My translation.
[98] Ibid., para. 504.

between mortals."[99] On an interpersonal level, the return of the soul in the relationship signals a relational bond that has attained a level of archetypal permanence: the feeling of connection endures, yet the conscious personalities remain free from inflation or projection. The relationship, now grounded in a deeper psychic reality, exists not in overt possession but as an impersonal, symbolic presence in the background of consciousness.

Plate #10: The New Birth

The final image in the *Rosarium Philosophorum* series commented upon by Jung depicts the "Rebis" (from the Latin *res bina*, meaning "double matter"), now resurrected and standing upon the moon. The accompanying verse proclaims: "Here is born the noble Empress / The Masters name her their daughter. / She multiplies herself / bears

---

[99] Ibid., para. 500.

children without number / infinitely pure / and without spot."[100] The emphasis here is on the feminine or anima side of the transformed being. The solar, animus counterpart of the Rebis is celebrated in image 17, which leads to the final descent into the grave of the unconscious as the green lion devours the sun (image 18). This is succeeded by the coronation of the Virgin in the celestial realm (image 19) and, ultimately, the appearance of the triumphant, risen Christ in consciousness (image 20).[101] Collectively, the *Rosarium Philosophorum* sequence allegorizes the individuation process: beginning with the initial, cautious encounter between conscious and unconscious and leading to their eventual union and full transformation. All of this is interpreted by Jung in his final and most elaborate work on alchemy, *Mysterium Coniunctionis*.

Image 10 represents the first true approximation to the final goal of the alchemical *opus*. Jung wrote that this image evokes a sense of eternity and immortality within consciousness—an impression that emerges from contact with the transcendent Self. In analytical psychology, this moment corresponds to the formation of the ego–Self axis. When such a connection is established, the experience is of being in touch with what is immortal within. As Jung wrote:

---

[100] Ibid., para. 307. My translation.
[101] For a discussion of the twenty pictures in the *Rosarium Philosophorum*, see my essay, "The Marriage of Animus and Anima in the Mystery of Individuation," in *The Mystery of Transformation*.

The end of the poem hints at immortality—
at the great hope of the alchemists, the
elixir vitae. As a transcendental idea,
immortality cannot be the object of
experience, hence there is no argument
either for or against. But immortality as an
experience of feeling is rather different...
On many occasions I have observed
that the spontaneous manifestations of
the self, i.e., the appearance of certain
symbols relating therein, bring with them
something of the timelessness of the
unconscious which expresses itself in a
feeling of eternity or immortality.[102]

Jung concluded his essay with this summary sentence:
"The transference phenomenon is without doubt, one of the
most important syndromes in the process of individuation."
By "syndromes," he intended not a pathological condition,
but a constellation of psychological challenges—or
"problems"—which, in Jungian terms, serve as gateways
to greater consciousness. He thereby suggested that the
profound interpersonal dynamics activated within the
transference, whether in analysis or in any other relational
context, constitute a privileged opportunity to experience
the immortal in oneself and the other.

---

[102] Jung, *Mysterium Coniunctionis*, para. 531.

Lecture Six

The Culmination of Jung's Opus:
Mysterium Coniunctionis

In the concluding chapter of *Mysterium Coniunctionis*, Jung's final and most comprehensive work on alchemical psychology, Jung turned to the writings of Gerhard Dorn—arguably his favorite alchemical philosopher—to articulate key developments in the process of individuation. This chapter, titled "The Conjunction," summarizes many of the insights Jung developed over his nearly twenty-five years of alchemical study. In it, he discusses three late stages of the individuation process: 1) *unio mentalis*, 2) embodiment of *unio mentalis*, and 3) integration of the *unus mundus*. These stages represent successive states of consciousness, symbolically mirrored in the laboratory procedures of alchemy and richly illustrated in alchemical texts such as the *Rosarium Philosophorum* (as discussed in the previous lecture). Together, they delineate the culmination of the alchemical psychospiritual *opus*.

Jung's initial inspiration for writing *Mysterium Coniunctionis* was Karl Kerényi's *Das Ägäische Fest*

(1940), which commented on a pivotal scene from Goethe's *Faust II*:

> This book—my last—was begun more than ten years ago. I first got the idea of writing it from C. Kerényi's essay on the Aegean Festival in Goethe's *Faust*. The literary prototype of this festival is *The Chymical Wedding* of Christian Rosencreutz, itself a product of the traditional hierosgamos symbolism of alchemy. I felt tempted at the time to comment on Kerényi's essay from the standpoint of alchemy and psychology but soon discovered that the theme was far too extensive to be dealt with in a couple of pages. Although the work was soon under way, more than ten years were to pass before I was able to collect and arrange all the material relevant to this central problem.[103]

Jung approached the task of completing his work on alchemy and psychology with the utmost seriousness, and he regarded Goethe's *Faust*—and particularly *Faust II*—as a continuation of the alchemical tradition. Goethe himself had read some alchemical texts, including the writings

---

[103] Jung, *Mysterium Coniunctionis*, xiii.

of Paracelsus, and considered *Faust* the "great work" of his lifetime. He completed *Faust II* at the very end of his life, and it was the only one of his works about which he felt able to say, "It is finished." For Jung, *Mysterium Coniunctionis* occupied a similar position. It was his own *Faust II*, representing a culminating expression of his decades-long engagement with alchemy.

At the beginning of the book, Jung describes the alchemical *opus* as follows: "the alchemist saw the essence of his art in separation and analysis on the one hand and synthesis and consolidation on the other."[104] These two movements—separation and integration— also define the work of individuation. As early as 1916, in *"Septem Sermones ad Mortuos"* ("Seven Sermons to the Dead"), Jung had already outlined this structure. The process begins in the undifferentiated fulness of the *pleroma*, representing a state of primal disorganization. From this field emerges *Creatura*, the organizing principle of consciousness, which initiates the differentiation of elements into dynamic pairs of opposites. What follows is a necessary synthesis that can bring the hostile elements and qualities together into a new, stable state. However, this requires a force strong enough to mediate the polar tensions. As described in "The Psychology of the Transference" (see the previous lecture), this force is delivered by the Eros principle, which is integrative.

---

[104] Ibid., xiv.

Under its influence, the *opus* can achieve its final goal. Of course, Jung puts all of this into psychological terms, conceptualizing the psychological *opus* as a movement from a preconscious wholeness (potentiality) through the separation of conscious and unconscious systems and the differentiation of ego-consciousness, toward the reintegration of conscious and unconscious elements manifesting in a realization of the Self.

Dorn's Stages of the Alchemical Process

The initial condition of the alchemical *opus*, as described by Gerhard Dorn, is called *unio naturalis*—the original unity of "soul" and "body." In alchemy, this state corresponds to the undifferentiated mixture of materials (*prima materia*) within the *vas*. At this stage, there is no separation between liquid and matter. The contents of the *vas* are saturated and unified. The first operation is to separate this undifferentiated whole into its constituents of matter (body) and liquid (soul), through the application of heat, bringing the mixture to a boiling point.

The psychological rendition of this original state runs as follows. Soul can be translated as psyche, and body as both one's given somatic condition (the body as one experiences it) and one's sensate intake of the immediate environment of people and objects. Psyche is immersed in body; they are one. This is naïve realism in the philosophical sense. Psychologically, consciousness is primarily oriented toward the material world and

122

interpersonal relationships, with only minimal (or no) reflection on the psyche's contributions to this perception or an "inner world" of symbolic, imaginal, or spiritual dimensions. Reality is thus defined by the senses, and emotional life depends on one's relationships with others and objects. Consciousness may be intellectually stocked with analytical thoughts about material "givens," as well as aesthetic in its appreciation of color and form, but it is not spiritually attuned or aware of symbolic reality. These dimensions of experience, which rely on the participation of "spirit," are not directly accessible and thereby discounted, as they are beyond the reach of everyday consciousness. Furthermore, the mediating role of projection in the construction of reality is not considered. This is the "natural state" of mind that follows from a sensate experience of the world.

It should be noted, however, that *unio naturalis* represents a psychological development from a previous, unrelated state of mind. When an infant is born, it is not consciously related to its "body." It is *in* the body, but not consciously related to the body as an object, nor is it related to any other "object" in the surrounding world. It is one unto itself, with no awareness of the sensate world it will soon discover, let alone an attachment to objects in that external world. To achieve *unio naturalis*, it must become attached—united with the sensory world it experiences. This occurs first in the arms and at the breast of the mother, and later with other persons and objects. To become attached is a psychological achievement, and an important one developmentally. Usually, the brain's mirror neurons develop quickly, enabling the infant to establish affective bonds with the external world. In the absence of this mirroring function, the individual remains confined within a solipsistic universe and is unable to attain *unio naturalis*—the foundational state from which all subsequent psychological developments described by Dorn proceed. Instead, autism spectrum disorder may develop.

The alchemists worked within a tripartite philosophical framework, conceiving the human being as composed of body, soul, and spirit. In the state of *unio naturalis*, what is absent is spirit—the element that introduces archetypal images, symbolic meaning, and a sense of spiritual purpose in both the soul and embodied life. While conventional or culturally acquired versions of these archetypes may still appear, they will lack the vitality of authentic spiritual experience. The soul serves as the intermediary between body and spirit and is capable of uniting them within the field of consciousness.

Dorn taught that, at the outset, the soul has a natural tendency to unite with the body and the material world. Jung elaborated on this, describing it in terms of the soul's mythical descent and embrace of Physis, resulting in its entrapment within a fusional prison. Psychologically, this seduction by Physis is successful due to the immediate and compelling power of sensory and instinctual experience. The human being is biologically predisposed to fall for this seduction—a tendency likely rooted in evolutionary imperatives related to the survival of the species. In nature, attunement to bodily sensations and environmental cues—both opportunities and threats— is of critical importance. Thus, we see the infant sucking vigorously at the beloved breast of the mother without the slightest training or reflection. It unites with the mother instinctively, and this begins the formation of *unio naturalis*. The animating factor in this process is the soul, which leads the body into active engagement with the surrounding world. At this stage, soul "lies caught in 'the chains' of Physis."[105]

In the laboratory, this stage is reflected in the alchemist's strong motivation to engage passionately in the *opus,* as well as their intense fascination with the transformation of materials within the *vas.* In illustrations of alchemists at their furnaces, we see this absorption in their eyes as they gaze intensely into their flasks. For the alchemists who remained in a state of *unio naturalis*, the goal was the transmutation of base metals into material gold, motivated by a desire for great wealth. Such practitioners were considered low-grade alchemists who sold their souls for material gain. They were devoid of philosophical or spiritual depth. Their sole focus was the production of tangible gold.

We know the state of *unio naturalis* very well from our everyday, naïve mode if consciousness, particularly

---

[105] Ibid., para. 673.

as we carry out routine tasks that demand our careful attention to detail—cooking, cleaning, driving, repairing broken appliances in the kitchen, and even shopping. In such moments, we do not question the reality of the objects before us, nor do we reflect deeply on the spiritual value or meaning of our actions. We simply engage in the world as it presents itself, immersing ourselves in practical activity. This is *unio naturalis*—not philosophical inquiry, but the preparation of a meal for oneself or loved ones, to whom one is naturally attached. Of course, there are notable exceptions, such as the Buddhist monastic cook who, in the spirit of meditative awareness, whispers to himself, "Wash the rice like you were washing your eyes!" In fact, what is today called "mindfulness" aims at this very kind of conscious presence in daily activity. Yet such awareness points toward a more advanced stage in Dorn's system. In *unio naturalis*, we act instinctively, guided by impulse, sensation, and intuitive orientation, seldom pausing to reflect on the deeper spiritual or psychological dimensions of our behavior.

Dorn's Stage One: *Unio Mentalis*

If the initial stage is "natural," the subsequent stage is decidedly not. It requires what the alchemists called an *opus contra naturam*—a rigorous mental effort that resists the natural tendency to equate reality with the perceptions and demands of the body and the material world. In this phase, *unio naturalis* is dissolved through a process of separation, wherein the soul is extracted from the body: "She must be called back by 'the counsel of the spirit' from her lostness in matter and the world."[106] Once liberated, the soul becomes capable of uniting with spirit, giving rise to what Dorn terms *unio mentalis*. In the alchemical *vas*, this transformation is symbolized by the steam rising from the material base—with water (soul) and air (spirit) combining before condensing into droplets at the top. The inert matter that remains at the base signifies the abandoned body, now dead. "The aim of this separation was to free the mind from the influence of the 'bodily appetites and the heart's affections,' and to establish a spiritual position which is supraordinate to the turbulent sphere of the body. This leads at first to a dissociation of the personality and a violation of the merely natural man."[107]

In his commentary, Jung wrote: "Modern psychotherapy makes use of the same procedure when it objectifies the affects and instincts and confronts consciousness with them."[108] The goal of *unio mentalis* is "the attainment of full knowledge of the heights and depths of one's own character."[109] Dorn's first stage of development beyond *unio naturalis*, then, involves freeing the soul from the fetters of the body. However,

---

[106] Ibid.
[107] Ibid., para. 671.
[108] Ibid., para. 672.
[109] Ibid.

this liberation entails more than merely overcoming the demands of bodily impulses and emotional drives—as difficult and dissociative as that may be. It includes a fundamental shift in perception: a penetrating insight into psychological projections that shape both our constructed view of external reality and our internal self-concept. In this new state, the image one sees in the mirror is radically different from before. Freed from the influence of projections implanted by cultural conditioning, the ego gains access to a more authentic form of self-knowledge. However, this process of stripping away the veil of illusion is experienced as distressing and painful, as it entails a confrontation with the shadow. The shadow must now be included in the self-image.

Throughout the long course of individuation—the *opus*—we are continually called to retrieve our projections. If we can recognize the psychological drivers behind these projections—unresolved complexes rooted in childhood or traumatic experiences—we can, and will, attain a certain measure of self-knowledge, building toward *unio mentalis*. However, projection also arises from the archetypal layer of the unconscious, as we repeatedly cast archetypal images onto the relative surfaces of both ourselves and our environment. In *Aion*, Jung discussed the anima archetype as the great projection-creator symbolized by the Goddess Māyā in Hindu theology, who enshrouds reality in illusion. Through this process, we unconsciously embellish the world, seeing all kinds of things that are not *out there* but formed *in here* and projected onto the screen that our consciousness takes in. We put our feelings, wishes, hopes, and fantasies about things and people *out there*. We humanize animals, personalize our cars and houses, find demons and angels in celebrity figures, and generally believe the images we see around us. This creates a feeling of home—a cozy and familiar world in which we can live comfortably. However, it also creates a terrifying jungle of dangerous forces that lurk about in the dark or in the "other." To uncover this illusory fiction and see through it is a profoundly painful task—one we instinctively resist. Instead, we want to fall back into *unio naturalis*. In analysis, this is called regression.

This first stage in Dorn's alchemical process is enormously consuming, both energetically and temporally. It constitutes a lifelong endeavor that can never be completed, aimed at making the unconscious conscious. If successful, it overcomes illusions and internal divisions and results in the creation of interior oneness, *unio mentalis*. This wholeness includes not only shadow and anima, but also the heights and depths of spirituality. On this, Jung commented: "The spirit (*animus*), which is to unite with the soul," Dorn calls "a 'spiracle' (*spiraculum*) of eternal life, a sort of 'window into eternity' (Leibniz)."[110] From this passage, it becomes clear that Jung's concept of spirit (animus) extended far beyond mere intellect, referring

---

[110] Ibid., para. 670.

instead to the human capacity to engage with *Logos*—a principle articulated in biblical, Gnostic, and ancient Greek philosophical traditions. This function manifests through the imagination, which serves as the conduit to all-encompassing, intuitive knowledge. Philosophically, it corresponds to the tradition of idealism, which holds that the foundation of reality is spiritual, not material.

Jung emphasized the role of imagination, and particularly active imagination, in the formation of *unio mentalis*. In his own experience, he found that active imagination offered one of the most direct and penetrating means of accessing the innermost recesses of the psyche. Through this method, the ego encounters the symbolic background of the unconscious, populated by figures that Jung called sub- or supra-personalities. These autonomous inner characters represent aspects of the unconscious that ordinarily remain outside conscious awareness. By actively engaging in dialogue with these figures, we may discover our inner world and discern its relationship to our conscious perceptions and attitudes. This deepened form of engagement may enrich the content of *unio mentalis*, as *The Red Book* testifies. In this book, we see Jung dialoguing with archetypal figures and giving form to these encounters through paintings, drawings, writings, and reflections. These visual and textual expressions serve not only as a record of his inner journey, but also his method of integrating elements of the collective unconscious into his evolving *unio mentalis*, as symbolized by his many mandala images.

Unio mentalis is also exemplified in the wisdom traditions of the East, where it is cultivated through disciplined practice over a long period of time. It is not the result of a singular mystical breakthrough, but the fruit of sustained inner work. To reach this level of development, a "higher power" is needed, and that is the "spirit."

Dorn's Stage Two: Creation of the *Caelum*

The second stage in Dorn's program involves the reunification of *unio mentalis*—the refined union of soul and spirit—with the inert body that was left behind during the soul's prior ascent. Thus, this stage represents a symbolic rebirth. Recall image 7 of the *Rosarium Philosophorum*, which depicts the hermaphroditic body (*unio naturalis*) in the grave, while the soul ascends heavenward. In Dorn's framework, this moment signals the creation of *unio mentalis*, occurring in the celestial realm where soul and spirit unite. In the subsequent *Rosarium Philosophorum* images, rain falls to purify the body, followed by the soul's return to reanimate it. The result of this process is the emergence of the upright and fully conscious "Rebis." This reintegration of the soul-spirit unity (*unio mentalis*) into the body constitutes Dorn's second stage, giving rise to what Dorn calls the *caelum*. The *caelum* is a subtle, luminous substance— a mysterious, air-like liquid of exceptional purity—produced through the alchemical procedures of refinement and repeated distillation, in both the library

131

and the laboratory. Jung identified Dorn's *caelum* as the *lapis philosophorum*.

The *caelum*, a most precious substance, represents the culmination of the *opus*. It symbolizes the integration that follows the initial separation of soul and body—one that is not merely conceptual, but also embodied. While the first stage creates a mental attitude (*unio mentalis*), the second stage grounds this spiritual attitude in lived reality. One might say the first stage yields theoretical or "head" wisdom—knowledge gained through mental processes such as reflection, active imagination, and meditation— while the second stage constitutes the enactment of that wisdom within the context of everyday life.

This back and forth movement between the mental and the practical is an important aspect of the individuation process. As Jung repeatedly claimed, individuation is not something one does sitting alone on a mountaintop or in a cave. Rather, it is forged in the midst of ordinary life—in relationships, family, and work. The wisdom gained must be tested, applied, and proven in the realities of the world. The *caelum*, in this sense, must demonstrate its authenticity through repeated trials. It is only through numerous experiments and inevitable failures that the true *caelum* emerges as the verified and incorruptible product of the *opus*.

This work of embodying *unio mentalis* requires tremendous conscious discipline, and must be regarded as an ethical undertaking. Ethics, in this context, refers to the practical application of principles and values gained through reflection and insight (*unio mentalis*). It is concerned with integrity—with the challenge of living one's paradoxical wholeness authentically in the world. Importantly, this second stage of the *opus* unfolds alongside the gradual development of *unio mentalis* over the course of a lifetime. One need not attain complete mental integration before beginning to embody one's insights. Rather, each emerging realization can be acted upon, allowing the individual to live with increasing consciousness. As previously described, these first two stages yield what Dorn called the *caelum*. Jung characterized this as the realization of the Self: the integration of opposites into a conscious and meaningful expression of the total personality.

For Jung, the human personality contains an infinite and godlike core—something transcendent, lying beyond material and historical existence. One cannot fully experience this in all its dimensions, but one may glimpse it through numinous experience. The sense of transcendence that is experienced in such moments, accessed through imagination and lived through ethical practice, is the *caelum*.

Dorn's Stage Three: Union of *Caelum* and *Unus Mundus*

The third and final stage in Dorn's alchemical process is the union of the fully integrated body-soul-spirit composite—the *caelum*—with the *unus mundus* ("one world"). The *unus mundus* is often conceived of as the primordial world—the condition of unified being that existed on the first day of creation. Basically, it is the unity underlying the manifest world—a world otherwise made up of discrete and separate entities. It is the invisible cosmic order that structures both the psyche and the cosmos. To unite the *caelum* with the *unus mundus* is to bring the microcosm of the realized Self into conscious relationship with the macrocosmic totality of existence. This union is most vividly encountered in the phenomenon of synchronicity. Thus, union of the *caelum* with the *unus mundus* amounts to living consciously in a synchronistically organized world. This represents the highest stage of individuation: the mystical stage. Jung described it as follows:

> If Dorn, then, saw the consummation of the *mysterium coniunctionis* in the union of the alchemically produced *caelum* with the *unus mundus*, he expressly meant not a fusion of the individual with his environment, or even his adaptation to it, but a *unio mystica* with the potential world.[111]

Here, the potential world refers to the undivided totality present at the beginning, before the world was split

---

[111] Ibid., para. 767.

into distinct parts, and the *unio mystica* refers to deep engagement with the divine. Jung wrote that "the idea of the *unus mundus* is founded on the assumption that the multiplicity of the empirical world rests on an underlying unity."[112] This unity is reflected in the causal connection between psyche and body, and, on a more profound level, in moments of synchronicity.

While working on *Mysterium Coniunctionis*, Jung was simultaneously engaged in dialogue with the physicist Wolfgang Pauli, exploring the intersections between depth psychology and quantum physics. Jung understood synchronicity as the empirical manifestation of the *unus mundus*—a moment when the hidden unity of reality momentarily appears in the empirical world of the foreground. Although the *unus mundus* remains essentially transcendental and beyond full comprehension, it occasionally reveals itself in subtle, suggestive ways. These glimpses—or hints—are synchronicities.

This corresponds to Dorn's third stage, in which the microcosm of the individual is linked to the macrocosm of the cosmos. At this point, the personal and the transpersonal are no longer experienced as separate but are integrated into a single, living unity. Stage three is thus a recognition of unity, and a full participation in this primordial wholeness. As Jung wrote: "this would consist, psychologically in a synthesis of the conscious

---

[112] Ibid.

with the unconscious."[113] For Jung, the unconscious is cosmic in scope—an unfathomable expanse that extends beyond the boundaries of the individual psyche.

The result of this final *coniunctio*—the union of a known quantity (consciousness) with an unknown one (the unconscious)—is, as Jung acknowledged, theoretically inconceivable. Yet in practice, it produces shifts in consciousness as far-reaching and transformative as those occasioned by the emergence of quantum physics from classical paradigms. Through this analogy, Jung suggested that, through investigation and penetration into the unconscious, we have arrived at a point where the synchronistic convergence of the individual and the cosmic becomes apparent. The material and psychological worlds, though seemingly distinct, appear to be meaningfully connected—and both are grounded in a third, unifying principle, the *unus mundus*. Awareness of this ground as a lived experience constitutes the mystical apex of Dorn's third stage.

This union—of Self and *unus mundus*, individual and God—is echoed in mystical traditions across cultures and epochs. The testimonies of mystics from both Eastern and Western traditions, both ancient and modern, affirm the profound subjective significance of such experiences. Jung suggested that, although this *coniunctio* defies rational comprehension, it manifests universally—in

---

[113] Ibid., para. 770.

alchemical symbolism, religious mysticism, and modern depth psychology alike.

Conclusion

Jung's writings on alchemy were not historical investigations. Rather, he approached alchemy as a symbolic resource and a link to other spiritual and philosophical traditions rooted in the Western imagination, reaching back to the pre-Gnostics. To establish a solid ground for depth psychology in the modern world (which was increasingly abandoning mythological and naïve dogmatic religious belief systems), alchemy proved key. Jung did not want human beings to be left without spiritual resources, which he regarded as fundamental to human existence and to a meaningful life. At the same time, he did not want to deny the value of modernity, as often occurs in traditional religious contexts. For Jung, Dorn's three stages of the alchemical process provided a perfect model for articulating the culmination of the individuation process as understood in analytical psychology.

Bibliography

Edinger, Edward. *The Anatomy of the Psyche: Alchemical Symbolism in Psychotherapy.* Chicago: Open Court, 1985.

Eliade, Mircea. *The Forge and the Crucible: The Origins and Structure of Alchemy.* 2nd ed. Chicago and London: University of Chicago Press, 1978.

Freud, Sigmund and C.G. Jung. *The Freud/Jung Letters: The Correspondence Between Sigmund Freud and C.G. Jung.* Edited by William McGuire. Princeton, NJ: Princeton University Press, 1974.

Gieser, Suzanne. *The Innermost Kernel: Depth Psychology and Quantum Physics. Wolfgang Pauli's Dialogue With C.G. Jung.* Berlin, Heidelberg, New York: Springer, 2005.

_____. ed. *C.G. Jung. Dream Symbols of the Individuation Process. Notes of C.G. Jung's Seminars on Wolfgang Pauli's Dreams.* Princeton, NJ: Princeton University Press, 2019.

Grotstein, James S. Foreword to *The Psychopathic Mind: Origins, Dynamics, and Treatment,* by J. Reid Meloy. Northvale, NJ: Jason Aronson, 2002.

Hakl, Hans Thomas. *Eranos: An Alternative Intellectual History of the Twentieth Century.* Translated by Christopher McIntosh. Sheffield, UK and Bristol, CT: Equinox, 2013.

Henderson, Joseph L., and Dyane Sherwood. *Transformation of the Psyche: The Symbolic Alchemy of Splendor Solis.* London: Routledge, 2003.

Hillman, James. "The Suffering of Salt." In *Alchemical Psychology.* New York: Spring Publications, 2010.

Jung, C.G. (1953–1983). *Collected Works of C.G. Jung.* Edited by Sir Herbert Read, Michael Fordham, Gerhard Adler, and William McGuire. 21 vols. Princeton, NJ: Princeton University Press, 1953-1983.

_____. *Aion: Researches Into the Phenomenology of the Self,* in *Collected Works,* vol. 9, part 2. Princeton, NJ: Princeton University Press, 1968.

_____. *Collected Works of C.G. Jung, Supplementary Volume A: The Zofingia Lectures.* Princeton, NJ: Princeton University Press, 1983.

_____. "Commentary on 'The Secret of the Golden Flower,'" in *Collected Works,* vol. 13. Princeton, NJ: Princeton University Press, 1967.

_____. *Memories, Dreams, Reflections.* New York: Vintage Books, 1961.

_____. *Mysterium Coniunctionis: An Inquiry Into the Separation and Synthesis of Psychic Opposites in Alchemy,* in *Collected Works,* vol. 14. Princeton, NJ: Princeton University Press, 1970.

_____. "Paracelsus as a Spiritual Phenomenon," in *Collected Works*, vol. 13. Princeton, NJ: Princeton University Press, 1967.

_____. "The Philosophical Tree." In *Collected Works*, vol. 13. Princeton, NJ: Princeton University Press, 1967.

_____. "Problems of Modern Psychotherapy," in *Collected Works*, vol. 16. Princeton, NJ: Princeton University Press, 1966.

_____. "Psychological Commentary on *The Tibetan Book of the Dead*," in *Collected Works*, vol. 11. Princeton, NJ: Princeton University Press, 1969.

_____. *Psychology and Alchemy*, in *Collected Works*, vol. 12. Princeton, NJ: Princeton University Press, 1968.

_____. "The Psychology of the Transference," in *Collected Works*, vol. 16. Princeton, NJ: Princeton University Press, 1966.

_____. *The Red Book: Liber Novus*. Edited by Sonu Shamdasani. Translated by Mark Kyburz, John Peck, and Sonu Shamdasani. New York and London: W.W. Norton & Company, 2009.

_____. "Septem Sermones ad Mortuos." Appendix 5 in *Memories, Dreams, Reflections*. New York: Vintage Books, 1961.

_____. "The Spirit Mercurius," in *Collected Works*, vol. 13. Princeton, NJ: Princeton University Press, 1967.

_____. "The Visions of Zosimos," in *Collected Works*, vol. 13. Princeton, NJ: Princeton University Press, 1967.

Kerényi, Károly. *Das Ägäische Fest: Erläuterungen zur Szene "Felsbuchten des Ägägischen Meers" in Goethe's Faust II.* Wiesbaden: Limes Verlag, 1941.

Lindsay, Jack. *The Origins of Alchemy in Graeco-Roman Egypt.* New York: Barnes & Noble, 1970.

Marlan, Stanton. *The Black Sun: The Alchemy and Art of Darkness.* College Station, TX: Texas A & M University Press, 2005.

_____. *C.G. Jung and the Alchemical Imagination: Passages into the Mysteries of Psyche and Soul.* London: Routledge, 2021.

McGuire, William. *Bollingen: An Adventure in Collecting the Past.* Princeton, NJ: Princeton University Press, 1982.

McLean, Adam. *The Rosary of the Philosophers.* Edinburgh: Magnum Opus Hermetic Sourceworks, 1980.

Meier, C.A., ed. *Atom and Archetype: The Pauli/Jung Letters 1932-1958.* Princeton, NJ: Princeton University Press, 2001.

Newman, K.D. "The Riddle of the Vas Bene Clausum." *The Journal of Analytical Psychology* 26, no 3, 1981.

Nietzsche, Friedrich. *On the Genealogy of Morals.* Translated by Walter Kaufmann and R.J. Hollingdale. New York: Vintage Books, 1967.

Shamdasani, Sonu. *C.G. Jung: A Biography in Books*. New York and London: W.W. Norton & Company, 2012.

Stein, Murray. "The Faith of the Analyst." In *The Collected Writings of Murray Stein: Volume 4: The Practice of Jungian Psychoanalysis*, 239-57. Asheville, NC: Chiron Publications, 2022.

_____. "Individuation and/vs Enlightenment." *The Mystery of Transformation*, 219-236. Asheville, NC: Chiron Publications, 2022.

_____. "The Marriage of Anima and Animus in the Mystery of Transformation." In *The Collected Writings of Murray Stein: Volume 8: Psychology and Spirituality*, 215-55. Asheville, NC: Chiron Publications, 2024.

Von Franz, Marie-Louise. *Die aesthetischen Anschuungen der Jliasscholien (im Codex Ven. B und Townleianus)*. Dietikon, CH: Buchdrückerei Oscar Hummel, 1943.

_____. *Book 2: The Passion of Perpetua: A Psychological Interpretation of Her Visions*, in *Volume 6 of The Collected Works of Marie-Louise von Franz: Niklaus Von Flüe And Saint Perpetua: A Psychological Interpretation of Their Visions*. Asheville, NC: Chiron Publications, 2022.

_____. *Aurora Consurgens*. Princeton, NJ: Princeton University Press, 1966.

_____. *Alchemy: An Introduction to the Symbolism and the Psychology*. Toronto: Inner City Books, 1980.

_____. *Muhammad ibn Urmail's "Hall AR-Rumuz": Historical Introduction and Psychological Comment.* Egg, CH: Fotorotar AG, 1999.

www.ingramcontent.com/pod-product-compliance
Lightning Source LLC
Chambersburg PA
CBHW020614270326
41927CB00005B/332